THE PSYCHOLOGY OF
ABORTION

GINETTE PARIS

Translated from the French
by Joanna Mott

SPRING PUBLICATIONS, INC.
PUTNAM, CONNECTICUT

Originally published in French in 1990 as *L'Enfant, l'amour, la mort*
by Editions Nuit Blanches. First published in English translation in 1992
by Spring Publications as *The Sacrament of Abortion* (ISBN 0-88214-352-2).

Published by Spring Publications, Inc.
28 Front Street, Suite 3
Putnam, Conn. 06260
www.springpublications.com

Inquiries should be addressed to:
Spring Publications, Inc.
P.O. Box 230212
New York, N.Y. 10023

Printed in Canada

Second Edition 2007

Design by white.room productions, New York

Library of Congress Cataloging-in-Publication Data

Paris, Ginette, 1946-
  [Enfant, l'amour, la mort. English]
  The psychology of abortion / Ginette Paris ; translated from the French by Joanna Mott. — 2nd ed.
    p. cm.
  Rev. ed. of: The sacrament of abortion. Dallas, Tex. : Spring Publications, 1992.
  Includes bibliographical references.
  Translation of: L'enfant, l'amour, la mort.
  ISBN 978-0-88214-560-0 (pbk. original : alk. paper)
  1. Abortion — Religious aspects. 2. Abortion — Moral and ethical aspects. I. Paris, Ginette, 1946 -
    Enfant, l'amour, la mort. II. Title.

HQ767.2.P3713 2007
363.46 — dc22

                          2007008212

♾The paper used in this publication meets the minimum requirements of the American
National Standard for Information Sciences — Permanence of Paper for Printed Library
Materials, ANSI Z39.48-1992.

CONTENTS

Introduction

5

A Brief History of Contraception and Abortion

11

She Has a Strong Heart

25

Women's Stories

53

INTRODUCTION

The wild one

I have drawn inspiration throughout this book from a guiding image, the Artemis of Greek mythology (known to the Romans as Diana). She is an untamed goddess, a champion of what we would think of today as ecological values. I have chosen her to enrich these reflections on abortion because her myth is full of what appear to be contradictory elements, the same kinds of contradictions that abound in considerations of abortion. Artemis is both a protector of wild animals and a hunter who kills them with unerring aim. How can the same divinity be the patron saint of hunters and the protector of animals? Greek women invoked her name during the pains of labor, but if a woman were to die or the infant could not survive, then a quick death, considered preferable in Greek eyes to a long agony or a life of suffering, was also attributed to Artemis.

The same goddess thus offers both protection and death to women, children, and animals. Why these contradictions? Why are they personified in a feminine divinity? Is it a way of saying that a woman's protective power cannot function properly if she does not also possess full power, namely the power over death as well as life? Her image belongs to us as well as to antiquity because, like all fundamental images of the human experience, which C. G. Jung called "archetypes," she never really ages but reappears in different forms and different symbols. So we may ask ourselves what is happening today to this archetype that combines in such a paradoxical way the love of life and the acceptance of death. She encourages us to become more aware of the power of death, its inescapable nature, and its necessary role in a living ecology. Abortion is about love, life, and death.

Why go back to mythology?

Mythology tells us what it's like to be human. We're all born of parents who become our principal divinities for a considerable period of our lives. Sooner or later we all have to detach ourselves and take up our own struggle against the forces of evil. We're all confronted with the mystery of the other sex and the mystery of nature. We all have responsibility for the generation that preceded us and the one to follow. Towards the end, after a life full of adventures (inner and outer), we try to make sense of it all, and then we die. This is what mythology is all about: images and stories that symbolically represent what is universal in human life. It is an expression of how reality appears to us, not an explanation, as science is. Mythology is so fundamental to humans that every culture without exception develops its own. Ours is expressed today through literature, film, television, advertising, fashion, song. It is revealed in the people we choose to honor, the stars that command our attention, in the economic, political, and cultural decisions we make. In short, mythology is to culture what dreams and symbols are to the individual. No one can survive without dreaming (awake or asleep) and no culture can endure without myths. This is what the mythologist Joseph Campbell meant when he said that a myth is a collective dream, whereas a dream is a personal myth.

How can a myth be changed?

We play many roles on the inner movie screen of our personal myth — hero or heroine, victim or savior, child or parent, shy maiden or brave knight, mother figure or old wise man. These are archetypal roles; that is, they are basic to our psychological being. Archetypes are at the foundation of every myth, personal or collective; they include ideas, emotions, attitudes, values, and behavior, and C. G. Jung called this entanglement of levels a "complex." These complexes, or archetypes, make up our basic scenarios. The proliferation of popular psychology books dealing with complexes of all kinds shows how hard we try to become aware of these scenarios so as to distance ourselves from roles that are no longer appropriate.

Judeo-Christian mythology has had the major influence on our Western culture for over two thousand years, providing ideas, values and symbolic images. Can we erase two thousand years of monotheistic influence by dropping all religious practice and declaring ourselves free of our parents' faith? Certainly not, as has been proved by our sudden awakening to ecological values.

We're only beginning to understand how a religion that strips nature of its sacredness so as to place everything sacred in one god (whose realm is not of this world) can be dangerous for trees, animals, oceans, forests, and body-consciousness, all of which were considered receptacles of the divine in polytheistic antiquity. It's not that simple to leave Judeo-Christian mythology behind because we have no idea to what extent it lingers in our subconscious notions of good and evil, in the choices we make, which on the surface have nothing to do with religion. It is still active in our most intimate emotional reactions, when feelings of anguish or guilt rise up suddenly without our knowing why. Our attitudes towards abortion are subconsciously stamped by Judeo-Christian values, even among those who consider themselves completely liberated from them.

We are now on the threshold of a liberalization of attitude towards abortion that is, in many ways, comparable to the freeing up of sexual attitudes thirty years ago. When contraceptive methods became more widespread after World War II it seemed like the end of sexual repression and Victorian values. Sexual attitudes underwent a complete reversal, and a new myth appeared in films, in literature, and in advertising in which women became more sensual and reclaimed the right to sexual pleasure without having their morality called into question. But women (and also the men who urged them on) found out that giving themselves permission was not enough to guarantee their pleasure. "Relax and enjoy it" was not that easy, even if that was precisely what was most wanted. It is a basic premise of psychotherapy that it is difficult to change any psychological reality as long as it remains unconscious. It controls us without our knowing it. Becoming aware of what controls us is the major key to healing in all therapeutic approaches. If women couldn't easily let themselves go, it's because of lingering unconscious prohibitions. The psychology of sexuality came a long way in half a century partly because a great deal of attention was paid to it. Reproductive morality does not fascinate us in the same way that sexual morality does. Once contraception and then abortion became acceptable we haven't given it much more thought, and the result is that the Judeo-Christian myth surrounding abortion is still with us, albeit on a subconscious level.

My use of pagan mythology in these pages is meant to provide contrast. When compared to the mythology of patriarchal monotheism, it becomes clear that there is more than one way to define morality, human dignity, children's rights, and the collective responsibility for life and death issues. It is also clear that all of this is intimately connected with global ecology. I will now return to the pagans to highlight what is still Judeo-Christian within us.

One among many

The choice of one goddess out of the incredibly rich assortment in Greek mythology requires an explanation. Why Artemis and not another? Many other divinities could be invoked in connection with ecology or abortion. Despite twenty years of acquaintance with these gods and goddesses of our pagan past, each time I put my attention on one alone I feel uneasy. They're all important, especially the overall richness of their relationships; each is part of a team, part of a never-ending group dynamic. Artemis, for example, has sisters, brothers, aunts, and uncles — all as important to the whole as she is. It was the Greeks' way of saying that reason (Apollo) is as important as emotion (Dionysos), that war (Ares) is as ever-present as love (Aphrodite), that a child needs a father (Zeus) and a mother (Demeter), that a husband needs a wife (Hera), that stability (Hestia) is as crucial as change (Hermes), that the sun (Apollo) needs his sister, the moon (Artemis) — in short, that each divinity, each archetype, represents a piece of human experience, and that it makes no sense to wonder which — head or heart, heaven or earth, feminine or masculine, sun or moon — should dominate the other. Greek mythology is a complex system in which there is room for everyone and everything, as long as a certain equilibrium is maintained and certain territories are respected, symbolized by the battles and the love affairs of the gods. The divinities make love to create new principles, they struggle and oppose each other to delineate their zones of power and to preserve their rights. Their unbelievably petty quarrels represent the in-fighting that goes on in our own consciences between opposing values. We, too, must juggle the same principles in the conduct of our own lives, and that's not an easy task.

But it's impossible to deal with the whole pantheon at once; sometimes at a party we feel like moving off in a corner to pursue a conversation with one person. It's in that sense that I restrict myself here to speaking with Artemis, wanting to examine in depth her point of view, but with full respect for the others.

This little book develops the idea that abortion is a sacred act, that it is an expression of maternal responsibility and not a failure of maternal love. If the issues surrounding life and death and children and love are not religious issues, or at least spiritual ones, what is left that is religious? But if we accept abortion as a religious act, then many questions arise. What sort of religion do we mean? Who defines it? What values does it represent? Judeo-Christian values, which may have seemed necessary, perhaps even redemptive, some 2,000 years ago, now appear more and more irresponsible, and I will try to show how they are infinitely more cruel than abortion. What is a moral stand on reproduction worth if it doesn't take responsibility for the children born of a religious duty? What kind of a pope (*el Papa* in Italian) invests in Wall Street instead of providing for the hungry and destitute? What kind of fundamentalist morality turns its back on the suffering of mothers and couples and children when babies arrive unwanted in the world? And, above all, can we accept any kind of religious morality that has lost sight of the larger implications of a global ecology?

A BRIEF HISTORY OF CONTRACEPTION AND ABORTION

Women have always been concerned with limiting births, long before over-population became a problem. Even in the most repressive societies, even at the risk of their lives, they found ways to practice contraception and abortion, which, in fact, have proved to be more of a religious problem than a technical one. In the beginnings of civilization, the Hebrews had already discovered the fertile days in a woman's cycle and that knowledge was used to increase fertility. In Greece, the priest-physicians in Hippocrates's school of medicine had to take a solemn oath (the famous Hippocratic oath) not to provide any woman with an "abortion pessary." That tells us that abortion pessaries existed, and that women had to ask someone other than a doctor to get one! In imperial Rome, a commentary by Juvenal reveals that then, as now, abortion was easy for rich women to obtain and difficult for poor women. "The common women, at least, accept the dangers of childbirth, and the fatigue of nursing an infant. Their poverty obliges them to. But on the gilded beds scarcely a woman in labor is to be seen, such is the effectiveness of procedures and drugs that make women sterile and kill the babies in their mother's womb."[1] But the example set by the ruling class is always contagious, and it's reasonable to assume that poor women also took contraceptive measures and were given abortive herbs by midwives, only with more difficulty and risk.

The Romans, Hebrews, Celts, and early Germans allowed a woman a certain amount of control over her fertility, thanks to the help of midwives, even though women were subordinated to men and valued mainly for their re-

---

[1] Juvenal, 6.592–96, in Guy Fau, *L'Émancipation féminine à Rome* (Paris: Les Belles-Lettres, 1978), p. 22.

productive capacities. Midwives, from the earliest times, have always advised women on all questions having to do with childbirth, nursing, contraception, and abortion. In the Middle Ages, this brought them the hostility of the Church. In an attempt to keep mothers away from them, the Church forbid the use of traditional remedies that eased the pain of childbirth, claiming that the desire to ameliorate such suffering contradicted the will of God. Mythology, as usual, served as justification: when God banned Eve from Paradise, did he not lay a curse on her and her descendants, namely, to suffer when bringing forth children? The desire to ease this pain is therefore an offense against God and, consequently, midwives should not help women. Priests took this curse seriously: in 1591, a Scots noblewoman, Eufame Macalyne, was burned alive for having asked a midwife for drugs to ease her labor pains.[2] Until the end of the nineteenth century, priests discouraged doctors from studying the causes of puerperal fever, the major cause of death among new mothers, because the Church considered these deaths an expression of God's judgment or punishment for some hidden immorality.

When chloroform and ether were discovered and the physician James Simpson proposed to use them in cases of difficult labor, the Church once again raised a hue and cry. A Protestant minister in New England wrote, for example: "Chloroform is an instrument of Satan who appears to offer women a blessing; but in reality it threatens to harden society and deprive God of the deep and urgent cries of women who call on him for help in their time of need."[3] One wonders where the Church Fathers got the idea that women's anguished cries were pleasing to God, a pleasure that mustn't be taken from him. It was Queen Victoria, puritan though she was, who finally silenced the Churchmen when she allowed her doctor to administer chloroform during the birth of her eighth child. When a Queen speaks, God speaks. The Church changed its attitude immediately, allowing the Queen to interpret God's will in her own way.[4] But it is as queen, not as woman, that Victoria won the day. The suffering of ordinary women hadn't managed to arouse the

---

2 See Andrew White, *A History of the Warfare of Science with Theology in Christendom* (New York: George Braziller, 1955).

3 Georges Vetter, *Magic and Religion* (New York: Philosophical Library, 1973).

4 See Barbara G. Walker, *The Woman's Encyclopedia of Myths and Secrets* (New York: Harper & Row, 1983).

compassion of Churchmen, but the reprimand of a powerful monarch got through to them.

Despite Church bans and the often violent repression of women and midwives, the history of the Middle Ages shows that couples took the risk of practicing contraception and abortion because they couldn't leave the number of births to chance. A study of birth and death registers by the historians Bonnie Anderson and Judith Zinsser shows that in 1427 in Tuscany, Italy, for example, the number of children per family corresponded directly to the economic curve and existing survival conditions.[5] A poor couple living in the mountains generally had one child during their marriage. A more prosperous couple living on the plains could afford an average of three or four. Families limited births by means permitted by the Church, namely, by marrying late or not at all. Thus, beginning in the ninth century, the census in Germany shows only 28.6% of the population marrying. In the north of France, at Saint-Germain-des-Prés, it was 43.9%; at Saint Remi de Reims, 33.4%. Couples took in adult brothers and sisters on condition they would not marry, so as not to divide the property.

By the end of the sixteenth century statistics are more numerous and more precise, and they demonstrate how the age at which people married affected the curve of births and corresponded exactly to the existing economic situation. In the English village of Colyton, for example, from the sixteenth to the nineteenth century, the average age for marriage goes from twenty-seven years in 1560 to thirty in 1647, dropping back to twenty-five around 1837, reflecting once again the prosperity curve of the times. Similarly, the average marriage age in a Tuscan village between 1650 and 1750 went from twenty-one-and-a-half to twenty-six-and-one-tenth. Irish families at the end of the nineteenth century continued to make their own choices: typically, one boy and one girl in each family had the means to marry, the daughter having to wait until she was thirty, the son twenty-eight, which tended to limit even further the number of births.

When the couple finally married and births still had to be controlled, they had to practice abstinence, for coitus interruptus or any other means of birth control were sinful. Even within a legitimate marital relationship, a sexual

---

5 Bonnie S. Anderson and Judith P. Zinsser, *A History of Their Own* (New York: Harper & Row, 1988), p. 137.

act that prevented procreation was called "fornication." Saint Augustine and Thomas Aquinas both condemned the practice of coitus interruptus despite the priests who came to the defense of the poor, pointing out their need to limit births so as not to sink more deeply into poverty. In 1930, Pope Pius XI forbid contraception in any form despite popular opposition. The position of the Protestant Church was the same as the Catholic Church until the twentieth century, but today most Protestant denominations, fundamentalists excepted, consider contraception to be a moral question for the individual. Fundamentalists of the three great contemporary monotheistic religions — Christianity, Judaism, and Islam — are all opposed to contraception, abortion, and the sexual autonomy of women.

Nevertheless, couples, and women especially, have consistently disobeyed Church doctrine ever since the end of the Roman world and the beginning of Christian sexual repression. Apart from marrying late or not at all, women have never stopped using contraceptive methods that they found effective: a cervical cork made of beeswax or a piece of cloth, drinking very cold liquids, remaining passive during intercourse, holding their breath, hopping in place after the man's ejaculation, vaginal douches or oral potions made of rosemary, coriander, willow leaves, balsam, myrrh, cloves, parsley, animal urine, or vinegar. Peasant women used salt, honey, oil, tar, lead, mint extract, and cabbage seeds for douches or as purgatives, believing them to be effective as spermicide. Ingesting lead or ergot could make a woman permanently sterile, but only at the risk of damaging her health and sometimes losing her life. Still, women continued to use these methods, along with the notorious needles or crochet hooks, which were used to open up the cervix to trigger an abortion, causing millions of women to bleed to death.[6]

When all of the above failed and the unwanted child was born, it was not unusual to send it away to a wet nurse in another locality; if family finances then became too tight, the family "forgot" to send the agreed-upon fee to the nurse who later informed the parents of the death of their child. This practice

---

6 These incredibly dangerous practices still prevail in many countries. One can read, for example, in *Preventing Maternal Deaths* (eds. Erica Royston and Sue Armstrong, World Health Organization, Geneva, 1989, p. 125) that in Bangladesh an abortifacient might contain quinine, potassium permanganate, ergot, or mercury, while in Malaysia pills made from lead oxide and olive oil are seen in the market stalls.

not only avoided the need to confess an infanticide but made the whole affair less painful, thanks to a kind of psychological detachment from the child taken away at birth. These children abandoned to nurses and then forgotten were mostly girls who would have required dowries and couldn't work the land as well as boys. Girl babies were also neglected by reducing their nursing time at the breast, which often brought on illness and death.

The evidence for this kind of selective infanticide[7] is seen in the disproportionate number of girls living in Europe between the ninth and seventeenth centuries. In normal times, men and women are about even in number in their youth. Normally, the balance would change later in life as men died in large number in wars and crusades, leading to a larger proportion of women in old age. When we see, for example, a case such as Saint-Germain-des-Prés in the ninth century, a highly-populated area, where there was a ratio of 100 women to 115–117 men, we must suspect that the practice of infanticide has affected the statistical norm. The lower one goes on the socio-economic ladder, the more this ratio is outside the norm, reaching 100 women to 133 men in an English village in the fourteenth century. For the year 1391–92, a list of serfs born on and attached for life to the property of John of Hastings in the south of England shows 46 women for 78 men! By contrast, during a prosperous period in the thirteenth century when a peasant couple could feed more children, the population grew accordingly and the ratio of women to men became almost equal.

No one will be surprised to learn that the Catholic Church chose to ignore this practice, not because it agreed to give couples (much less women) a certain amount of freedom in these matters, but because it was not without guilt itself. During the eighteenth and nineteenth centuries the Church was overwhelmed with the responsibility for babies and children left on the steps of churches. Many of these babies were sent to wet nurses (only the older ones were kept in orphanages). But no one in the Church worried that the mortality rate of the babies left with underpaid or unpaid nurses reached almost unbelievable proportions, up to 75% in the nineteenth century! These nurses, poverty-stricken themselves, let the babies die when the Church stopped the payments. Rather than open up its coffers, the Church turned away. Rather than giving women

---

7 J. Hufton and S. Langer, "Infanticide: A Historical Survey," *History of Childhood Quarterly*, Vol. 1, No. 3 (Winter 1974).

the means of controlling births, it turned a blind eye to the results of its ideal principles. Children died of starvation and the nurses were assumed to be incompetent. The babies could die as long as they were baptized!

Nothing has changed, really. Today, pro-life groups within and without the Catholic Church pay scant attention to the misery of abandoned children, despite slogans and messages of love to the contrary, and they are prepared to sacrifice the lives of women. They ignore the fact that every year, worldwide, an average of 200,000 women (especially poor women) die as a result of clandestine abortions, according to a very conservative report issued by the WHO.[8] To get an idea of the scope of this indifference, let's multiply

---

8 *Preventing Maternal Deaths,* p. III (note: this publication is available at the Pan American Sanitary Bureau, Regional Office, World Health Organization, Washington, D.C. 20037–2895). To be precise, as of about 1980, the annual number of abortion-related deaths in certain developing regions was estimated at 204,450. This figure is believed to be conservative since it is based on hospital admissions for abortion complications. It is well-known that in many cases the woman dies without even a chance to seek help.

This statistic only includes developing regions (Latin America, Africa, Southeast Asia and Oceania, Southwest Asia, and South Asia). One can read in the WHO report that, in Latin America, complications of illegal abortions are thought to be the main cause of death in women between the ages of fifteen and thirty-nine. The rate of abortion among women over thirty-five is twice that for women aged twenty to thirty-four (p. 110), which means that most deaths occur among young mothers who already have three to five children. Between ten and thirty percent of the beds in obstetric and gynecological wards of most Latin American hospitals are filled by women suffering abortion complications. The Catholic Church undoubtedly still plays an important role in helping to maintain restrictive abortion legislation and in attempting to ensure that abortion services are unavailable, yet the Church appears to have little or no practical influence on the attitudes of individual women with unwanted pregnancies (p. 119). Reports from many developing countries cite abortions as one of the underlying causes of maternal death, if not the main one (p. 110). The number of annual deaths due to backstreet abortions used to be much higher. Since the legalization of abortion in many countries, there has been a radical diminution in the number of accidents although no statistic is available from the past. But given the estimated 40 to 60 million abortions that take place every year around the world and knowing that backstreet abortions present a risk of death 100 to 500 times greater than the medically safe procedures, one can imagine what the number of annual deaths was before the legalization of abortions in many countries.

this number by the forty-six years since the end of the war, when the massacre of 6 million Jews horrified the whole world, and justifiably so, leading people everywhere to examine their consciences. After forty-six years, these 200,000 women sacrificed annually make a total of 9,200,000 women. Do these unnecessary deaths shock the Church? No, because these women are considered immoral and unclean, as was said of Jews. They committed the sin of abortion and got what they deserved. Christianity, Judaism, and Islam are murderous religions for women, and I wonder what world court will have the courage to denounce it, as we denounce other human rights abuses.

Let's recall a few simple facts
The universal desire among women to control births expresses today, as it always has, the knowledge that survival depends on the ability to give each child what it needs for its full development, whether it be the survival of a mother, a family, or a community. Mothers are the first to know this because they are, everywhere and always, the first to suffer from scarcity and the first to see their children suffer from it. In research carried out around the world in an effort to understand the ravages of hunger, illness, and poverty, one fact remains constant: everywhere, and in whatever context, women and children are the first to be affected when resources become scarce or are concentrated in the hands of a privileged few.

Today this typically feminine awareness must extend to humanity as a whole: we are beginning to understand collectively that the continued availability of our planet's resources depends on our ability to slow down the population explosion. The reasoning is the same at the global level as with the individual mother who knows she can't allow herself to produce another child without endangering the health of the ones she already has.

In a book published in 1984, Pranay Gupte, then research director of the UN Fund for Population Activities, after visiting fifty countries, concluded

---

What is even more, the number of 200,000 deaths a year does not take into account maternal deaths at childbirth or weeks after delivering a child, in all those cases where a pregnancy was predictably fatal due to poor health, malnutrition, or absence of medical facilities for high-risk cases. The estimated number of maternal deaths in developing countries (p. 31) is thought to be about 500,000 women a year — almost all could have been prevented with proper care, contraception, and safe abortions.

that women want less children, but men want more because they want more sons.[9] Men's motives range from the most elementary and stupid kind of machismo, unfortunately very widespread, to a desire for security in old age, with tribal and national pride somewhere in between. Since it is men who control governments, the author says, the Third World still sees increased population as a sign of strength for a nation because that mentality is deeply rooted in men's minds. He recalls the first world conference on population held in Belgrade in 1964, when the combined strength of the triple alliance, namely the Third World, the Catholic Church, and the Communist Bloc, opposed the population control proposals put forth by the United States. In the twenty years since then, the rulers of Third World nations have been forced to realize that more people mean simply more mouths to feed, and not more riches. But at the level of the family the attitude remains the same; the patriarch wants many sons and will not give his wife any freedom of choice. Gupte, who also studied the "One child per family" program in China, concludes that draconian measures will have to be imposed on populations refusing contraception and that these measures must include, as was not the case in China, community-wide education and reflection on the rights and obligations connected with procreation.

I happened to be visiting Caracas, Venezuela, the week after a visit by Pope Jean Paul II. The Church's message of "go forth and multiply" coupled with its restrictions on contraception suddenly struck me as unbelievably cruel in a city where the numbers of abandoned children increase every year, abandoned by mothers who are themselves poor and exhausted. The cruelty of the message is all the more refined as it is presented under the guise of love. The rich in Caracas, as almost everywhere, have access to contraception and can hop a plane to the States for an abortion. Was the Pope talking to the poor, already so destitute that they abandon their children? Their suffering is obvious; how many children mistreated, abandoned, or even shot are needed to open his eyes?

Today the UN estimates a total of 100 million homeless children — children without parents, money, or education. And the fundamentalists of every stripe still preach "Go forth and multiply," as a message of love! Until some-

---

9 Pranay Gupte, *The Crowded Earth: People and the Politics of Population* (New York: Norton, 1984).

one decides to send them the bill or the children themselves, they will not get the point. These leaders behave like irresponsible men who can never quite pay child support for their children but who buy themselves a luxury car and a fancy condo; they need it, they say, to polish their image and do business. They find quite natural to let the mothers and the State look after the children! Children are not on their minds There is only one cure for that kind of irresponsible behavior: to send them the bill or, even better, the children themselves, to love and care for.

Neither the Churches nor the politicians care about children; they don't care about mothers; they don't care about tensions in local communities or the implications of overpopulation for global ecology. At the root of patriarchal religions is the need to control the bodies and souls of women. The minute women are set free, their institutions crumbles. It is a fact of history. The leaders know it.

Sociological research has revealed the connection between overpopulation and ecological disaster. Many reports from different disciplines show the relationship of overpopulation to the abuse of resources, the crowding into ghettos, and the increase in suicides, rapes, and domestic violence. And again, coming full circle, domestic violence leads to absent fathers, abandoned women and children, increasing poverty. In fact, overpopulation is the most inhuman of scourges because it turns us against each other and destroys all respect for life. In this context, the so-called humanitarian message of fundamentalists of all faiths is very ironic: produce babies even if they die of hunger, forbid abortion but don't give women what they need to feed the children they produce. Dogged by their shadow, the leaders refuse to realize that 95% of the billions of people who will be added to the world population will be born in the poorest countries, the ones already suffering from hunger. These are the same hunger-driven countries that presently cut down their forests, abuse their natural resources, and will eventually turn into desert the land that might have nourished them. We may well ask, along with the ecologist John Livingston, to what banquet Pope Paul VI invited the world's children when in 1965 he begged the United Nations not to support population control so that all unborn children might be allowed to participate in the "banquet of life?"

Consider the following figures: between the year 1 AD and 1650 the rate of growth would anticipate a doubling of population in 2,000 years. The plague was then a powerful controlling agent. Between 1650 and 1850, in 200 years rather than 2,000, the world population doubled again, and yet again in the 100 years that followed. Today it is estimated that the global population can double in thirty-five to forty years. What kind of power does the Church represent in this context? The pro-life message of love carries with it, for those who fall for it, a cruel reality — a brutal crowding together that robs everyone of his or her humanity.

Give us your sons!

Catholic priests used to teach that women who die in childbirth, along with soldiers who die in wartime, can go straight to heaven without confession. Today Islamic leaders guarantee their soldiers a place in Allah's paradise if they die in a holy war against the devil. (The devil may take the form of American capitalism or women who refuse to submit to the absolute authority of men). This guarantee seems all the more manipulative as it is often directed to very young adolescents, barely out of childhood, who don't really understand the nature of their sacrifice. But if the horrors of Islamic fundamentalism are obvious, our own history of intolerance and the effect it has had on our culture are more easily overlooked. The Judeo-Christian fundamentalist has killed and continues to kill in the name of the faith. The victims are women and children, whose suffering fails to attract the media in the way that military action does. It is helpful to recall from time to time this catalog of intolerance. There are abundant examples from the beginning of the history of the Church to the present day.

A letter attributed to Clement (Bishop of Rome and fourth Pope from 89 to 97) mentions, for example, that anyone refusing to bow his head before bishops and priests was guilty of insubordination and must be put to death.[10] Pope Innocent I, in the fifth century, proclaimed that God gave the Church the right to kill those who deviated from religious orthodoxy.[11] For two thousand years, the Church blessed mothers for giving life and soldiers (including the soldiers of Christ) for taking it! Equally important to remember are the following words spoken by Martin Luther, a founder of Protestantism:

---

10 Elaine Pagels, *The Gnostic Gospels* (New York: Random House, 1979).

11 V.L. Bullough, *The Subordinate Sex* (Champaign, Ill.: University of Illinois Press, 1983).

"If women become exhausted and die in childbirth, there's nothing wrong with that; let them die at the moment of birth, they were created for that."

One night I was watching a television documentary with my daughter, then fourteen years old, and we were both overcome by the scenes of warfare: children burned to death, peasants shot in front of their homes with their children as witnesses, young soldiers barely out of adolescence forced to dig their own graves and then lie in them and be stabbed to death with knives, military hospitals filled with hopeless amputees, orphanages full of sad-eyed children who have seen too much, mothers collapsing in grief at the news of another son's death, women who must look after husbands who left in health and returned disabled. My daughter watched this solemnly, realizing how imperfect life is, how lives are being destroyed en masse, everywhere, every minute.

The documentary was followed by a news bulletin; a reporter was interviewing a man who brandished a pro-life sign at a demonstration against abortion. The reporter, holding out the microphone, asked him why he was there. The demonstrator stated with much feeling that he was against abortion because it was a crime and an abomination, murder, in fact, to take the life of a human being, even at the fetus level. My daughter's reaction showed me how surprisingly sensible adolescents can be when they consider the adult world. She could neither understand nor accept that the horrors shown in the documentary were permissible legal actions sanctioned and funded by governments, forgiven and sometimes even blessed by the Church. To be allowed to kill men, women, and children who are full of life and fully conscious of suffering, a simple formula is needed — a declaration of war. These same men who decide whether or not to kill in war then dare to talk about crime and murder when a woman sacrifices a fetus no bigger than a raisin and less conscious than a chicken. [12]

---

12 Clifford Grobstein, an embryologist at the University of San Diego, has devoted more than ten years to the study of fetal reaction. His results have been published in *Science and the Unborn* (New York: Basic Books, 1988). He is presently a member of the ethics committee of two organizations established to discuss the abortion issue: the American Fertility Society and the Catholic Health Association. In the course of an interview for *Psychology Today* (September 1989), Elizabeth Hall asks his opinion, as an embryologist, about the pro-life propaganda movie *The Silent Scream*. He calls their interpretation of a twelve-week-old fetus's

When women decide to abort, it is for the sake of principles that are not that different from the ones invoked by the makers of war: freedom, self-determination, issues of dignity as important as one's own survival. The beings sacrificed in abortions do not suffer as do the victims of war and ecological disaster. The difference in thinking between the war maker and the anti-abortion demonstrator can best be explained by the division of power over life and death between men and women. Men have the right to kill and destroy and when the massacre is called a war, they are paid to do it and honored for their actions. It is sanctified, even blessed by our religious leaders. But let a woman decide to abort a fetus that doesn't even have the neurological apparatus to register suffering and people are shocked. What's really shocking is that a woman has the power to make a moral judgement that involves a choice of life or death. That power is reserved for men.

Any extreme contrast in gender roles implies a division of power between men and women that is absurd for both sexes: woman as life-givers, men as war heros, purveyors of death. In this kind of distribution women have the power to give life and no right to destroy it, whereas men are absolved from killing but are dissuaded from loving life, women, and children too much. It is expected that a woman will love and care for all the children that her biologic destiny imposes on her, and that a soldier will be able to kill without flinching. When this kind of polarization is found within a couple, it's definitely a sign that something is wrong, that the two partners are in an unhealthy situation, because the ideal of infinite compassion and generosity in women is as untenable as the perpetually strong and warlike aggressiveness of men. When this polarization spreads throughout a culture, warlike aggression reaches its peak.

The collective unconscious has always used different ways to reduce the population when resources and space are lacking or when the social climate deteriorates. War is obviously the cruelest means; it occurs inevitably when populations expand dramatically. Overpopulation leads to war, to violence, to the abuse of children; that is a constant in history. Lives are sacrificed by men rather than by women. But in war, the power of death is unleashed in all its fury, beyond rationality. War is much more irrational and excessive than

---

reflex movement as pain "pure fantasy" because the neurological apparatus responsible for what we call pain is not yet formed in the brain.

exercising the right to abort, and it has been in the exclusive hands of men for far too long. We've become so accustomed to thinking of war as normal that we've lost sight of what it costs in human feeling to give birth to, to raise and to love a child with one's whole heart only to offer it up as cannon fodder. In this context, the return of the ancient goddess Artemis invites us to imagine a new allocation of life and death powers between men and women, an allocation that allows men to appreciate the cost of a life and women to make decisions based on their maternal knowledge.

SHE HAS A STRONG HEART

Who is Artemis?

At least a head taller than the nymphs with whom she shares the forest, the goddess Artemis is represented clothed in a short tunic, revealing long athletic legs. Daughter of Leto and Zeus, and twin sister to Apollo, her symbols are the crescent moon, the doe, the she-bear, and the mare. She lives in the wilderness and, unlike Apollo, is not attracted by city life or the pleasures of civilization, marriage, or sexuality. Fiercely independent, she is a virgin living in the deep forest. The Romans portrayed her as Diana, the Huntress.

She is in charge of the woodlands and prairies where

> no shepherd dares to feed his flock within it:
> no reaper plies a busy scythe . . . [13]

What we now call a virgin forest was once called a forest of the Virgin, that is, a forest dedicated to Artemis. She was protector of a wilderness that, like herself, has never known man. To the ancient Greeks it was very important that such places existed and that humans could learn to regard them as places to be revered rather than resources to be exploited.

Her mother Leto searched desperately for a sheltering place when she felt the birth of her child approaching. She looked everywhere, but humans hesitated to help her, fearing the vengeance of another goddess, Hera, queen of heaven and wife to Zeus. Hera wanted to prevent Leto from delivering a

---

13 Euripides, *Hippolytus,* trans. David Grene. In *Euripides I,* eds. David Grene and Richmond Lattimore. The Complete Greek Tragedies (Chicago: University of Chicago Press, 1960), 75–76.

child fathered by her unfaithful spouse. Finally Leto found refuge on the isle of Delos where the people accept her and where her first child Artemis is born. The birth is painless and Artemis immediately begins to take care of her mother who suffers nine days and nights of labor before delivering the twin Apollo. Vengeful Hera has prevented Eileithyia, the midwife to goddesses, from attending Leto. Artemis never forgot her mother's suffering and devoted herself to relieving the agony of women in labor: "I hear women in the throes of labor crying for my help — the Fates made me their helper the moment I was born, because my mother felt no pain in birth or pregnancy." [14] Artemis also helped female animals to bear their young, and this knowledge gained in the forest made her, though a virgin herself, the guardian of women becoming mothers.

In his hymn to Artemis, the Greek poet Callimachus tells how she rebels against the idea of being a princess; she wants nothing to do with dresses or jewelry or anything that usually attracts a girl becoming aware of her femininity. What does she want then? Her father Zeus asks, wishing to give her a gift. She wants freedom! She wants to run in the mountains, swim in the river, ride horseback, chase after deer. Today we would call her a jock, or a tomboy, no longer realizing how perfectly normal that energy is in a young girl. And yet she is the quintessential *puella,* that is to say, the archetypal young girl. She asks Zeus if she can forego the long encumbering dresses worn by women, and their finery. She prefers the freedom of movement allowed by a tunic above the knee, along with solid unembellished sandals unlike the ornate ones worn by Aphrodite. Instead of jewels and fine clothes she begs for arrows and a quiver, like Apollo, and finally she asks to remain a virgin, which in Greek means "she who belongs to no man." Instead of a lover or husband she prefers a brotherly relationship. Artemis and Apollo — the twins, the moon and the sun — are equals and equally necessary to each other.

Young boys and girls around the age of nine, when they began to loosen their ties to their mothers, were dedicated to Artemis in a ritual ceremony. Adolescents stayed under her protection until they became citizens and spouses. On the eve of her marriage, a young Greek woman dedicated her short tunic and her playthings to Artemis.

---

14 Callimachus, "Hymn to Artemis." In *The Poems of Callimachus,* trans. Frank Nisetich (Oxford: Oxford University Press, 2001).

She shoots, she kills!

> Of Artemis, goddess with distaff of gold, whose cry resounds,
> I sing, the virgin revered, the archeress shooter of deer,
> The sister by birth of Apollo, god of the golden sword.
> In the chase over shadowy mountains and wind-swept peaks
>   she delights,
> And takes aim with a bow of pure gold, dispatching arrows
>   of woe.
> The heads of high mountains tremble, the thick-shaded forest
>   screams out
> A dire echo of bestial clamor, and shudderings shake both
>   the earth
> And the sea that is teeming with fish; but she with a heart
>   that is strong
> Now this way turns, now that, destroying the race of the beast.[15]

The Homeric hymn presents Artemis as an unerring archer and hunter. The hunt requires an alert consciousness, quick and agile reactions, and the capacity to take an animal's life without hesitation to stave off one's own hunger. A hunter has to predict what an animal's next move may be. A part of his mind belongs to his prey, because in order to outwit him he must know him intimately. The hunter of antiquity was not engaging in sport; he was feeding his own animal nature, and this in no way contradicted his love for the animal which would nourish him. The paradox of a goddess who hunts the animals she protects must be seen in this context. To grasp her state of mind we must realize that she loves the animal she pierces with an arrow.

Nature goddesses are sometimes linked to a kind of bucolic sentimentality, the belief in innate goodness championed by nineteenth-century romanticism and seen today in the resurgence of interest in forgotten goddesses. But there is more than one type of nature goddess. If, for example, one seeks the comfort of a mother's chicken soup or apple pie, then it's the image of Demeter, goddess of tilled fields and maternal generosity, that satisfies and not Artemis the hunter. The image of an ancient prepatriarchal matriarchy, snug as grandmother's house, does not jibe with the dark side of Artemis, symbolized by a crescent moon. Nor does it jibe with another lunar goddess,

---

15 *The Homeric Hymns,* trans. Michael Crudden. Oxford World's Classics (Oxford: Oxford University Press, 2001).

Hecate the terrible, who is the dark side of the moon, symbol of sorcery and magic. Both Artemis and Hecate, who is always clothed in black, have a harsh edge to them that rules out pastoral romanticism and balances out the generous side of the nourishing goddesses. There's no such thing as a good goddess and a less good goddess; each is an aspect of reality; in every religion that recognizes a maternal deity fostering life there's a complementary figure standing for death, ending, rupture. Mother Nature is both the giver of life and the taker of life, for there is no life without death. It is, therefore, appropriate to correct the too sweet and tender view of predominantly matriarchal religions by remembering that there is a fearsome aspect to women's fully developed powers.

Artemis had a reputation for liking bloody sacrifices, including human ones, from the earliest recorded religious history of Greece, a practice that has given paganism such a bad name. Jews and Christians like to think it was Jehovah who put an end to it when he restrained Abraham's arm and spared Isaac. But apparently the Jews have kept the tradition of human sacrifice going longer than the Greeks[16] and, furthermore, they forget to mention that the Greeks didn't have to throw out their goddesses in order to stop this practice. A certain ambiguity has implied that the feminine divinities had to be eliminated to stop the sacrifices. At the end of the fifth century BC, when Euripides wrote his two versions of the Iphigenia myth for the theater, a generation after Aeschylus's version, human sacrifice was already considered a bizarre and barbaric custom, which Greeks of the classic era could not relate to in any way.

The story of Artemis claiming Iphigenia as a sacrifice can be told and understood in more than one way. We will consider two versions: in one, Iphigenia is a victim, offered in sacrifice on the altar of Artemis; in the other, she becomes a heroine, and sacrifice takes on a different meaning.

Since abortion is a kind of sacrifice, I believe an exploration of this myth may open up fresh avenues of thought.

---

16 Franz Cumont, *Oriental Religion in Roman Paganism* (New York: Dover Publications, 1956), p. 119.

Iphigenia as victim

The adolescent Iphigenia is a daughter of Queen Clytemnestra and King Agamemnon, commander of the Greek fleet in the war against Troy. Here is the legend: Agamemnon has offended goddess Artemis and as divine punishment his boats are becalmed in port with no wind in their sails. Kalchas, a soothsayer, is consulted, who says the only way to resolve the problem is to sacrifice Iphigenia on the altar of Artemis, to appease her anger. The princess Iphigenia is at Mycenae with her mother Clytemnestra. Agamemnon, motivated by military ambition, or by his idea of the common good, or by Menelaus and Ulysses who are eager to set sail, agrees to sacrifice his daughter. He asks Clytemnestra to send Iphigenia to him, under the pretext of marrying her to the hero Achilles, but instead of a wedding celebration it's Kalchas's knife that awaits the youngest, and favorite, daughter of Clytemnestra. The mother sings wedding hymns happily, believing her daughter is being married whereas in fact they're about to slit her throat. But at the last moment the goddess substitutes a live doe for Iphigenia, and all's well that ends well, for Artemis carries her off to the land of the Tauris and makes her the priestess of her temple.

It's likely that Euripides was touched by this legend, which was already ancient when he made a drama of it. He wrote two versions. In the first, *Iphigenia in Tauris,* the girl is sacrificed *against her will* by the wild tribes of Tauris whom Euripides criticizes for their cruelty. One suspects Euripides cannot bring himself to present Artemis as a bloodthirsty goddess. After all, he lived at a time (480--406 BC) when the idea of human sacrifice was profoundly shocking. So he depicts the sacrifice of Iphigenia as a ritual that only barbarians (i.e., non-Greeks) could carry out. And he places the action in Tauris, where human sacrifices to a virgin goddess comparable to Artemis were offered.[17] He blames their cruelty on their barbarity, and wishing to defend the goddess, has Iphigenia say, "O Artemis, these people, being murderers themselves, are charging thee with their own wickedness. No, I will not believe it of a God!"[18] Euripides also insists on placing the legend at an earlier epoch, about seven centuries before his time, and makes that epoch a turning point

---

17 According to Herodotus, the first Greek historian and a contemporary of Euripides.
18 Euripides, *Iphigenia in Tauris,* trans. Witter Bynner. In *Euripides II,* eds. David Grene and Richmond Lattimore. The Complete Greek Tragedies (Chicago: University of Chicago Press, 1956), 388--91.

in changing attitudes. He tells the story, basically, of this shift in mythology, how the notion of sacrificing human beings became odious to humans as well as to the goddess.

Iphigenia as heroine

Several years later, Euripides returns to the same legend and writes a second version, *Iphigenia at Aulis,* in which Iphigenia is no longer a victim but a heroine. Her sacrifice is not imposed on her; it is accepted by her and even by her mother Clytemnestra. Euripides offers a feminine equivalent to the biblical scene when Abraham's arm is restrained by God at the moment of killing Isaac. Abraham's bloodthirsty God had been encouraging human sacrifice long enough for Abraham to believe that the sacrifice of his only son would be pleasing to him. The myth is modified when that kind of mentality changes so that God himself was seen as proposing a shift in attitude. When he restrains Abraham's arm, Jehovah states that he doesn't want to be honored in that way any more, and this scene marks an evolution in Judeo-Christian mythology. Similarly, the Greeks wanted to cleanse Artemis of her reputation as a bloodthirsty goddess, and this was expressed through the genius of Euripides. What's amazing is that religious history continued to present the Pagan as bloodthirsty while overlooking Jehovah's past. And yet, did not Artemis rescue Iphigenia? The scene that follows, described by Euripides, is certainly as explicit as the Bible story:

> . . . and the priest
> took up the knife,
> praying, and looked for the place
> to plunge it. Pain welled up in me
> at that, and I dropped my eyes.
> And the miracle happened. Everyone
> distinctly heard the sound of the knife
> striking, but no one could see
> the girl. She had vanished.
> The priest cried out, and the whole army
> echoed him, seeing
> what some god had sent, a thing
> nobody could have prophesied. There it was,

we could see it, but we could scarcely
believe it: a deer
lay there gasping, a large
beautiful animal, and its blood ran
streaming over the altar of the goddess.
Then Kalchas, with
such joy as you can imagine, shouted, "Commanders
of the assembled armies of Greece, look:
the goddess has placed this victim
on her altar, a deer from the mountains,
and she accepts this instead of the girl,
rather than stain her altar with noble blood.[19]

Like any other myth, Iphigenia's death can be interpreted in many ways. It can be seen as the sacrifice of a daughter to a father's political ambition. An "Agamemnon complex" thus expresses the situation of a father who is obsessed with power and ambition and not only fails to give his daughter the attention she needs but also uses her psychologically, as if her destiny only existed in relation to his success. We say currently when describing an ambitious man that he "sacrifices" his daughter or his family to his political or social aspirations. The fact that Agamemnon has no wind in his sails is also symbolic. For a man like him, career and business, which for him means war, come first. He will even sacrifice his child to get his warship moving and out to sea.

Another interpretation, more historical than psychological, might see this story as marking the point in time when the ancient matriarchal power of Mediterranean societies lost its authority. Clytemnestra's inability to protect her daughter may be seen as the decline of maternal power in favor of the father. Even when her own child is involved, Clytemnestra cannot, in fact, oppose the decisions made by her husband, who is now behaving like a master towards a slave. Iphigenia is Clytemnestra's favorite daughter, a darling child torn from her love. Agamemnon is behaving here like the classic dominating husband and father, and it's astonishing to realize to what extent the patriarchal culture that ensued will positively sanction this kind of abusive behavior. Clytemnestra, acting on her authority as queen and mother and evoking

---

19 Euripides, *Iphigeneia at Aulis,* trans. W. S. Merwin and G. E. Dimock, Jr. The Greek Tragedy in New Translations (Oxford: Oxford University Press, 1978), 2116–40.

her cultural background, where women had some power behind their pride, decides to avenge her daughter's death (as well as the affront of being replaced by Agamemnon's new wife). She kills him. But she is condemned by the morality of the time. The message is clear: a father's power, however unjust or abusive or even fatal, cannot be questioned by any woman, even a queen. And to make the point totally clear, Orestes, Clytemnestra's son and Iphigenia's brother, takes no part in avenging that death or in supporting his mother. He stands on the side of the father. Defending Orestes's matricide, Apollo calls on the sexist theory of his time, namely that a woman is merely the furrow that receives the male seed:

> . . . the so-called mother of the child
> isn't the child's begetter, but only a sort
> of nursing soil for the new-sown seed.
> The man, the one on top, is the true parent
> while she, a stranger, foster's a stranger's sprout. [20]

This turning towards the patriarchal mentality in the classic period will later have its full development in Christianity and Judaism, when all the goddesses will have been effectively erased from mythology. Psychology, encouraged by the patriarchal spirit of the Freudian era, built a whole theoretical structure on the unbearable guilt of the son who kills his father (Oepidus) even though the act was unintentional, even though he didn't even know the identity of his victim. Completely overlooked is the equally fundamental Orestes complex, where the son destroys his mother, knowing exactly what he is doing, knowing also that the power of the throne will be his. Orestes, let's not forget, inherits political power by eliminating his mother. Several generations of psychologists have focused exclusively on the Oepidus complex, as if the Orestes complex were not every bit as basic.

But there's more to the myth than the loss of feminine authority. Like dreams, myths can be perceived in more than one way, and multiple interpretations may emerge, each one as valid as the next. We can see in this myth the defeat of women by the patriarchal spirit or we can look at it from Artemis's point of view and wonder why Iphigenia was offered to Artemis and not to

---

20 Aeschylus, *Eumenides.* In *The Oresteia,* trans. Alan Shapiro and Peter Burian. The Greek Tragedy in New Translations (Oxford: Oxford University Press, 2003), 769–73.

some other goddess, even though it may seem a roundabout way to get back to the theme of abortion. Abortion is so broad an issue, that many strange roads lead to it.

What is human sacrifice?

Polytheism was discredited by the image of an innocent child being dragged by evil pagans to an altar to be sacrificed to a cruel female goddess, as if God had not also demanded the sacrifice and crucifixion of his only son. The immolation of Christ is always presented as a redemption. But Euripides made Iphigenia a redeemer of Greece long before the myth of Christ as redeemer. He has her say,

> . . . I have made up my mind to die.
> I want to come to it
> with glory. I want to have thrown off
> all weak and base thoughts. Mother,
> look at it with my eyes,
> and see how right I am.
> All the people, all the strength of Greece
> have turned to me. All those ships,
> whether they sail, whether Troy falls,
> depend on me. I will be the one
> to protect our women, in the future,
> if ever the barbarians dare to come near. [21]

For Euripides, as for us, the sacrifice of a nonconsenting victim is murder. For Aeschylus, the Greek dramatist who preceded Euripides by forty-five years, it is clear that Agamemnon commits a crime if Iphigenia tries to escape. In his version of the story, Aeschylus has witnesses express horror that the victim is unwilling to die: Iphigenia had "her mouth gagged, the bit yanked roughly, stifling a cry that would have brought a curse down on the house." [22]

The fact that the witnesses are scandalized by her unwillingness to die shows us that ancient sacrifices, if they were meant to please the gods, had to be voluntary. The Greeks retained a revealing superstition from that: if an animal escaped the priest's knife it was considered a bad sign and the animal

---

21 *Iphigeneia at Aulis,* 1845–56.
22 Aeschylus, *Agamemnon,* in *The Oresteia,* 270–73.

was spared. When human sacrifice was acted out on the stage, the person went willingly to the altar; it was no longer murder but, more nearly, martyrdom. Iphigenia's behavior is thus related to the martyrs and virgins that Christians loved to extol for their courage. Since, in fact, we know very little about the era when human sacrifice was supposed to have taken place, it's very possible that the victims approached the altar like Christian martyrs: ecstatic, ready to meet their death.

It's true that the potential martyr is conditioned and manipulated by his or her culture. Clans, families, religious sects — from the Greeks and early Christians right up to the present — always exercise enormous psychological power when they convince their members that their credo is worth more than life itself, that one must die rather than abandon the faith, the cause, the totem, or the flag.

Before continuing with the theme of sacrifice I'd like to clarify a personal matter. Heroic self-sacrifice is hard for me to appreciate because as a child I rebelled when the nuns suggested that I meditate before a bleeding Sacred Heart, or a Christ on the cross, chest pierced through, nails tearing through flesh, forehead crowned with thorns. Nor did I appreciate the abundant details in literature, art and Christian mythology of the tortures suffered by martyrs — burned at the stake, stretched on a wheel, imprisoned, impaled, decapitated. When I began to study the Greek gods and goddesses their good nature seemed much healthier — up to the point where the character of Artemis made me reconsider the whole question. She is a pagan goddess, and yet she is the personification of absolute values, of purity at any price, a quality that leads inevitably to martyrdom. In this, Artemis is the opposite of beautiful Aphrodite who is so easygoing, so conciliatory, lending herself to any compromise that allows love and desire to triumph. But in Christian mythology there is no balance, and the tendency towards sacrifice takes on great emphasis for lack of a counterweight. In a polytheistic context one balances out the other, Artemis balances out Aphrodite. There are mothers (Gaia, Rhea, Demeter) and non-mothers (Athena), lovers (Aphrodite) and wives (Hera), young virgins (Artemis, Iphigenia, Persephone) and old maids (Hestia).

As Christ begs his father not to spare him, Iphigenia is also eager to sacrifice herself. She says to her mother,

> I say what I am about to say
> with no regard for anyone . . .
> Let me save Greece if that is what I can do.[23]

Her death will assure the salvation of all of Greece and her act will redeem
the transgressions of Agamemnon and the betrayal of Helen. Iphigenia hon-
ors the god who demands the sacrifice of her life, as Christ did, and like
him on the Mount of Olives she weeps for the last time before receiving her
martyr's crown. Unlike the Christian myth, however, it's a goddess and not a
god who exacts her sacrifice, and her anguish at having to die is addressed to
her mother and not her father:

> Mother, why these tears for me? . . .
> No more of that. Do not take
> my own courage from me . . .
> The altar of the goddess, the daughter of Zeus,
> will be my grave. Tears are forbidden there . . .
> Now there must be no tears.
> And you, young women,
> join in my hymn to Artemis the virgin,
> and celebrate my fate.[24]

The spirit of sacrifice and the desire to live on in memory are the same.

Christianity: a sacrificial religion

When I tell my students that the priests in ancient Greece sacrificed animals
on their holy altars, most of them perceive it as cruel. They picture a little
lamb being disemboweled on a stone altar by a priest wielding a big knife. To
them, pagans appear to have bloodthirsty tastes. But we must remember that
the Greeks only ate meat at celebrations and their way of apologizing to the
animal was to turn the killing into a ritual. Out of respect for animals, they
termed sacrifice what we've replaced with slaughter, an act of which we're not
even aware. Meat eaters do not care about finding out how the animals they eat

---

23 *Iphigeneia at Aulis,* 1919–26.
24 Ibid., 1942–97.

are killed, nor about the refined cruelty of the new methods designed to keep meat tender for gourmet dining (like keeping a calf for its entire short life in such a narrow space that he can't stand up so that his muscles will not harden). The Greek ritual of offering a portion of the animal to the gods also served as a way to avoid wasting the fat and bones, less attractive for human consumption, while the faithful (and especially the priests) treated themselves to the meat. Once we've admitted that we, too, sacrifice animals we may wonder, do we also sacrifice humans? No! Certainly not, it's a crime in our books. But if we ask, do we waste human life? The answer to that is more complex.

Judaism and Christianity presented human sacrifice as a phenomenon of the ancient goddess religions, as if such barbarity was due to the presence of feminine figures in the pantheon of gods, as if the patriarchy was alone in opposing such a squandering of human life. But that is simply not true. Every culture, whether it be matriarchal, patriarchal, ancient or modern, has a certain way of sacrificing human life. It is sometimes difficult to detect in our own culture because we develop airtight rationalizations to avoid seeing it. Neither patriarchy nor Christianity have really put an end to self-sacrifice for religious, ideological, or political ends. What has changed are the causes and the way it is done. We have our own martyrs but the form, the meaning, and the people officiating are no longer the same.

From the little we know about ancient sacrificial practices, the victim seems to have been killed for no apparent reason except that a god asked for it. In contrast, our customs take on an elaborate rational reasoning, which eventually arrives at a legal or religious judgment by which we are then permitted to destroy, torture, or lock up people in the name of political or religious ideals. We have taken more lives in the name of faith, race, regime, party, or progress, relatively speaking, than the archaic societies sacrificed to their most bloodthirsty gods. According to a very conservative estimate, the number of pagans massacred in the Holy Wars, the Crusades, and Inquisitions was a thousand times greater than all the Christians massacred for their faith or condemned by the Roman emperors. [25]

---

25 Homer Smith, *Man and His Gods* (Boston: Little, Brown and Co., 1951). See also Robin Lane Fox, *Pagans and Christians* (New York: Knopf, 1987).

The Béziers massacre in France is a well-known example of the Christian propensity to sacrifice human lives when orthodoxy is threatened. Here is the story: in the Middle Ages, when the Cathars were being persecuted in the south of France, the town of Béziers was attacked by the King's army, allies of the inquisitors who wanted to punish the Cathar heresy. Once the town was taken, the commanding general put the following question to the inquisitor, a Dominican priest: how could they tell heretics from good Christians within the civilian population? The inquisitor, in a celebrated reply, said, "Kill them all, God will recognize his own!" In this one massacre, more people were killed than in the most publicized persecutions of Christians by whatever pagan emperor one cares to choose. But it did not get the same attention as those Christians who were thrown to the lions because they refused to accept the Roman law of submission to the emperor.

Anthropological studies of archaic societies often count the executions of convicts and prisoners of war as human sacrifices when the death ritual implies an offering to a god. But let us not allow words to obscure the truth. In our culture, the most sophisticated public rituals surround the sentencing process (investigations, arrests, interrogations, trials, or mock trials) and the sentences are lived out far from the public eye. We no longer see the suffering of the condemned. In Western countries, where capital punishment still exists, the actual putting to death is reduced to a formality in front of a few witnesses, mostly minor officials paid to carry out the sentence. In archaic societies, the most elaborate rituals attended the moment of death in a solemn, public ceremony. So it is our judicial system that is heavily ritualized, not the actual carrying-out of the sentence. But suffering is there, even if we are no longer allowed to see it. Every culture has ways of controlling, punishing, or killing off those individuals who do not respect the values on which it has been founded. My intention is not to compare the respective merits of the treatment of criminals but to qualify what we mean by human sacrifice. Once that point is made I want to consider the values that underlie our sentencing procedures, because it seems that we live in a culture that, on the pretext of preserving life, tends to sacrifice mothers.

The wasting of human beings
The Christian martyrs enjoyed acclaim to the extent that the spiritual values they defended were esteemed. To die for one's faith was a big deal. But when

we shift to the value placed on life today, we may wonder in what category to place the 114 million children who, according to a 1989 UNICEF report on the situation of children in the world." suffer from adult violence, hunger, torture, prostitution, and illnesses due to unhealthy environment. Of that number 14 million die each year, according to UN figures. Not to mention the young people who die of drugs before our eyes with such regularity that these deaths can hardly be called accidental. How do we feel about the rise in suicides among the young and the elderly, which we know are caused by an ensemble of psycho-sociological conditions that can be modified? And what of the millions of lives attributed to the smoking of tobacco when medical research has long since proved its destructive effects? Why do we still refuse to impose standards of safety on automobile manufacturers, which we know would cost money but also save lives? How do we explain governmental tolerance of large industrial polluters whose damaging effects lead to fatalities? What does it mean that our governments support regimes that attach little importance to human life (especially the lives of women and children)? Why do we so easily accept political and bureaucratic decisions that in the long run deprive entire communities of what they need to survive? We sacrifice to the god of money, the god of progress, the god of power.

And, in another category of lives wasted, what are we to make, for example, of the racing car driver whose violent death is only a matter of time? He is no standard-bearer for a cause, he defends no collective values as might be expected of a martyr, but the spectacle of his death satisfies and absolves a need for violence among those who consider him a hero. And the more this kind of hero courts death, that is, takes risks, the more he is cheered. Of course, the word *accident* is used here rather than self-sacrifice, but would the public continue to support this kind of spectacle if it did not get its regular ration of deaths? The promoters think not, which is why they exploit the fatality statistics, the short life-expectancy of their racers, and the photographs of crashes that prove it's a serious business. For cultural reasons (and because we no longer kill with our own hands the animals we eat) the idea of a Roman gladiator's sword disemboweling his adversary shocks us much more than two automobiles crashing into each other. And yet a sizeable number of roman gladiators reached retirement age, and whereas some were forced into the arena, many others chose to do it on their own will, for the good pay, and all were trained under experts. Our so-called sports rituals (involving high risks and drugs) are as sacrificial as were the gladiators' combats: a certain number are certain to die.

Sometimes death is the best option

We can all imagine a circumstance in which we would be ready to give our lives for the sake of our child, our family, our freedom, or for a cause that seems more important to us than life itself (democracy, perhaps, or racial or sexual equality). The fierceness displayed by Artemis in defending her virginity is symbolic of the fact that certain values must absolutely not be betrayed or else our soul is violated, our identity extinguished, and we are haunted by our betrayal.

Heroic individuals have appeared regularly throughout history to the point where we may wonder if heroic self-sacrifice is not an integral part of the human condition. Iphigenia, Christ, the Japanese kamikazes, the Buddhist monk setting himself on fire, the political martyr, the Christian martyr, the mother who shields her children with her body, the father who pulls his family from a burning house — all put their lives at risk voluntarily and remind us that some values are worth the sacrifice.

Martyrdom, sacrificing for a cause, euthanasia, or heroic suicide that the media is so keen about — all these suggest daily that death, under certain circumstances, may be preferable to life. *Abortion always has been and continues to be another way of choosing death over life.* Aborting a fetus that is not welcomed is simply a shift of emphasis, for Christianity has always been a religion of sacrifice: it has sacrificed the mother rather than the child. Artemis's function is to protect the purity of life. The Pagan Virgin will not allow life to be diminished, wounded, or degraded in any way. The goddess who has the strength to support women as they give birth does not falter when, with her swift arrow, she provides a quick death.

The war between the sexes is a religious war

It's been said in more ways than one that the war between the sexes is first and foremost a religious war. This is more than obvious when we consider the choice of causes to which life is sacrificed and the way power is exercised in deciding who will be sacrificed. Those millions of women across the centuries who died while aborting in appalling conditions were truly sacrificed, the unwilling victims of sexist religious dogma. If the World Health

Organization estimates that 200,000 women die each year as a result of clandestine abortions, we may well wonder what the total figure would be for the last two thousand years of monotheism — be it Christian, Jewish, or Muslim. It's such an incredible figure that I get dizzy thinking about it. To the extent that these women did not sacrifice themselves voluntarily, like a mother intercepting the blows meant for her child, their deaths, in the ancient Greek mentality, would be closer to murder than to sacrifice. Today we cannot talk about accidents or acceptable risks because the technology of safe abortions has been available for a long time; it's a matter of a simple inexpensive procedure, safer than a vaccination. With the new French pill RU-486, it is no more painful than a normal menstruation cramp, and the cost is cheaper than pulling a tooth.[26] If women are obliged to seek out clandestine abortions and so many die from them, then it's clear that our religious morality and our political will are not concerned about the sacrifice of their lives.

The reason that questions about birth control, always of vital interest to women, have been handled so long in confessionals by an exclusively masculine clergy is because all biological and spiritual functions connected with women, and with a couple's sexuality, have been desanctified. For two thousand years Christianity has spurned equality between the sexes: women have neither a goddess in their image nor a priestess to serve them. Under these conditions it is not surprising that the conservative religions fail to see that birth control and abortion can be the expression of a highly evolved form of feminine consciousness and not simply an egotistical act. And the stability of the human community may depend on exercising and refining that awareness.

From a pagan point of view, it is quite stupid and even absurd to sacrifice a mother for the sake of a newborn because the child obviously needs her. Furthermore, in a culture where animal life and human life are seen as part of the same continuum, moral judgments constantly have to be made before killing an animal for food. When we kill in order to eat, we place a higher value on human life, and that is our justification. Artemis, who personifies

---

26 The so-called French pill, developed, in fact, by a team of Swiss and French researchers, is based on a hormone described as an anti-progesterone named RU-486. Believed to make most surgical abortions superfluous, it appears to be the safest method yet. The woman need only take the pill for two to four days, and the egg is expelled with little discomfort.

respect for animal life, accepts the necessity of the hunt, but only if the rules and the absolving rituals are observed. In most goddess religions a similar reasoning is applied to the fetus and the newborn. It is morally acceptable that a woman who gives life may also destroy life under certain circumstances, although there are restrictions on the use of this power, and there is always a time limit within which the decision must be reached. The amount of time varies in different cultures, but beyond that point whoever kills a fetus commits a murder. Today, in most countries where abortion is permitted, the taboo applies from the moment the fetus is normally viable but it is important to point out that in older cultures an infant was considered viable when its mother could nurse it, and it was given a clan and family name by its father, thus symbolizing a collective commitment to its future. *It is that commitment that we have lost.* We *know,* for instance, that many babies — victims of AIDS, malnutrition, maternal diseases, and addictions — will live just a few years at best. If the pro-lifers consider life to begin at conception, why not call these shortened lives, aborted lives? This time-delayed abortions are so unsurpassed in cruelty that they become totally unacceptable.

One evidence that fundamentalists do not care for the children is the latest example of Romania. As a result of the anti-abortion and anti-contraception laws, many children were forced on families who could not take care of them. After the fall of Ceauşescu, there was an estimated 100,000 children in orphanages that were severely underdeveloped, autistic, malformed, and undernourished as a consequence of their abandonment and the scarcity of the resources. (I do not include in this statistic the children who contracted AIDS as a result of receiving blood as a substitute for food). These are actually living miscarriages. Miscarriages of justice.

The gesture of arms extended to receive and bless one's children was symbolic of the mother goddess. The Catholic popes borrowed it from her cult. Menstrual blood was not a curse imposed on woman for her sins (and her femininity) as in Christian dogma. Far from being seen as an evil substance, it was considered to be endowed with magical powers. The popes, despite their open arms and compassionate expressions, despite their white robes, despite the chalice (once a symbol of goddess Demeter), have all missed the main point, something mothers have always known, namely, the survival and well-being of a child are linked to the well-being of the mother and to the capacity of the community to welcome them both.

In this context, the image of a pope extending a welcoming embrace is an illusion. The papal robes conceal an empty breast; his open arms take more than they give. Even though he dresses in robes, the clothing of women, and speaks of the Mother Church, the pope heads an institution that has systematically and very consciously desanctified all functions having to do with a woman's life cycle. This is why it is time to return to the symbolism of Artemis and all the other goddesses, each of whom represent an aspect of feminine consciousness.

Artemis stands for the refusal to give life if the gift is not pure and untainted, whether it be by the domination of one sex over another or by conditions that make it anything but joyful. A mother who never learns to say "no," "stop," and "enough" threatens her child's well-being; the same principle applies from the moment of conception. To say no is a fundamental aspect of being maternal. It is more than limit-setting. It is an insight coming from Artemis that "no" is fundamental to life and the survival of the planet. Those who claim that abortion today is an indication of selfishness on the part of women and couples, that the child is sacrificed to the lowest standards of our atheistic materialism, express a certain aspect of the problem because egoism and materialism certainly do exist. But by looking closely at individual cases, a more important theme emerges: the majority of women who abort do so because they know that the unwelcome child, born of constraint and misfortune, will be wounded in some unacceptable way. As Artemis might kill a wounded animal rather than allow it to limp along miserably, so a mother wishes to spare the child a painful destiny. There is nothing more cruel than the suffering of children, and mothers know this better than anyone. It is not immoral to choose abortion; it is simply another kind of morality — a pagan one. It is time to stop being defensive about it, time to point an accusatory finger at the other camp and denounce its own immoral stance.

Abortion is a sacred act

Attitudes towards abortion have become polarized since sexual morality lost a religious background. On the one hand, there are those who favor abortion, who see it as something *private* and *medical*, a matter of individual morality in which religion has no place. They overlook the fact that abortion often provokes an important *spiritual* crisis in women and within couples, a crisis that goes beyond the purview of the medical process. At the other extreme, the pro-lifers oppose abortion from a *religious* and *collective* point of view. In their eyes, no one has the right to abort, and their thinking is religiously based. In this case, the spiritual dimension is acknowledged but only within Christian dogma, as if no other form of spirituality existed. Obviously, everyone has a right to his religious beliefs, but what if mine are Pagan?

Christians: put your money where your mouth is!
Let's take the example of some pro-life parents who for religious reasons forbid their adolescent daughters to have abortions. No law makes them economically and morally responsible for the babies born of their minor children; in most cases these adolescents mothers and babies become dependent on the government, which may, on occasion, assume the cost of an entire lifetime — needless to say a thousand times more costly than an abortion. I wonder why we don't turn the argument back on those who won't support free abortion and let them pay for the consequences of a backward Christian morality. If parents object to an abortion for a minor child and they have the resources, why not make them take full responsibility for the infant? It is they and the fundamentalists churches who insist that the birth take place. Why not send them the bill? They need to have the courage of their convictions. Our religious leaders are not concerned with earthly affairs, which means that they pass the bill on to the State. And that bill is astronomical by comparison to providing free abortions.

The same irresponsible attitude exists in regard to prenatal diagnostic tests for serious congenital illnesses; the pro-life faction is opposed because the tests may lead to a decision to abort. Once again, it's the taxpayer that takes economic responsibility for children whose parents insist on bringing them into the world with infirmities, which will make them wholly dependent. Why don't we question the cost to the community of decisions that are based on personal religious beliefs?

Let me make myself clear. Never would I suggest that aid be refused to a family who is raising a child made dependent by an accident of nature. As long as these accidents are not predictable, like fire, flood, and other natural or biological catastrophes, the support of the government for families thus afflicted is a humanitarian act of which a nation can be proud. To lose this kind of security net would be a backward step. But as soon as an alternative exists, there is inevitably and immediately grounds for discussion. The parent then makes an informed choice, namely, to produce a child who will never be self-sufficient. In a democratic society, we would never force an abortion on a woman or a family who is morally opposed, out of respect for their religious beliefs. But to the extent that it is a private *choice* we can apply the same reasoning and ask who should be responsible for the costs. Is it the Church? The couple? The taxpayer? The woman alone? The local community? Private charity? At present the government underwrites the religious morality of the Judeo-Christian majority, at the same time proclaiming the separation of Church and State.

The same logic would apply to the father. No law so far has managed to make fathers really responsible for their paternity; many of them oppose contraception and abortion and, at the same time, act as if they were eternally celibate. The State, meaning you and I, pay a huge bill for this, not just in economic terms (it's well-known that the women most apt to turn to abortion are those who are economically deprived) but in social terms as well. It's rarely the religious institutions that serve as substitute father to these children abandoned by their natural fathers but the woman, her extended family, the school system, the neighborhood, the government, and in many cases the correctional system. Police officers trained to work in areas with a high rate of juvenile delinquency know that they stand in symbolically for this absentee father as well as for law and order. One of these officers wrote this comment at the end of a psychology paper:

> These youngsters seek us out and provoke us the way an adolescent provokes his father. They cut their teeth on us. We're very aware that we function as fathers, that the police officer is sometimes the only regular-type man that the kid may encounter in his life. The kids are always pushing the limits, and the officer must set the limits because there's no father around them to say "That's enough, kid." It's impossible to follow up on them individually, which is what's needed, and when they commit a subsequent offence it seems like they're asking for our attention. Most of these kids were not wanted, and they know it. Their mothers are worn out because they have to work and do everything at home as well. Their partners left them with the entire responsibility, material and moral. When their children become adolescents they become overwhelmed; that's when they fall apart. That makes the children very aggressive.

There's a difference between respect for the religious convictions of a minority — that is, to accommodate a social group that opposes abortion and refuses to practice it — and being forced as a community to take responsibility for their choices. Everyone has a right to his own moral choices, but when that means that women and the integrity of the social fabric and the planet itself have to bear the consequences of unwanted children, then we all need to be heard. It's perhaps a bit provocative to say, "I'm a pagan and my sense of what's moral isn't the same as Christian morality," but such a statement could make the point that Judeo-Christian morality plays a much larger role in public life than we suspect.

The first Christians refused a life that seemed to them a negation of love and justice. When a Christian chose martyrdom, he acted in the name of his spiritual life, and it was the purity of his commitment to human values that made him prefer death to a life of compromise. The same kind of thinking allows us to choose abortion when we are incapable of offering a child the best of ourselves and our resources. There's a threshold, both physical and psychological, beyond which we sense we cannot offer the gift of life. Giving life is the fairest of gifts; it cannot be given halfway. If we want to point the finger today at morally inacceptable behavior, it would be those persons who force others to reproduce without taking responsibility for the consequences. Maybe we should send all the unloved, undernourished, uneducated children — the battered ones, the prostitutes, the delinquents — to the patriarchs of all churches who forbid contraception and abortion to their wives, mistresses, daughters, or sisters. If they were truly held responsible for their religious beliefs, and if, in fact, they were required to assume full financial care and everyday moral support for these unwanted children, life on this planet would never be the same again. Doing a mother's job would automatically change their consciousness.

Anti-abortion groups impose their values on the overall community on the pretext of holding sacred religious beliefs. We can respond by invoking another moral standard, which is just as sacred — respect for the mother/ child connection. Because this relationship is the most intimate of all relationships and because a woman's womb is sacred, it is an unacceptable moral violation to force any woman to carry and raise a child against her will. It's a very serious matter to damage this sacred link right at the beginning of life because the seeds of bitterness are sown at a time when love and receptivity are called for. Forcing a child to live in a body that is hostile to it must be denounced as cruel. Is there a less promising way to come into the universe?

Life is too precious to allow sexist or religious hostilities to poison the very first stage. The purity of the child calls for an unmixed response on our part to bring forth each single one.

Women everywhere have always demanded the right to practice contraception and abortion. And it is women who spend the most time with children, loving them and caring for them. Everywhere in the world, poverty is a reality for women and, most particularly, mothers. Sociologists now use the expression "the feminization of poverty" to describe this development, which is observable worldwide. In 1981 Betty Friedan drew attention to the curious set of values held by the anti-abortion group lobbying in Washington at the time.[27] The same pro-life group that put the life of the fetus ahead of the mother's life in the so-called Amendment for Human Life also proposed to reestablish the law allowing fathers physical control (corporal punishment) over wives and children in the Laxalt Family Protection Act. This attitude is a basic tenet of fundamentalist Christian, Islamic, and Jewish monotheism.

These monotheists refuse to admit the fact that it's the child who is the first to suffer when there's no room at home, when the exhausted or abused mother no longer feels she can give of herself, when the resources at hand, despite everyone's best efforts, cannot guarantee the bare minimum of care, space, attention, and the love that every human being must have to survive intact.

Child against mother

In the case of difficult births, Catholic priests have, in the past, been under orders to sacrifice the mother's interest to the child's, and those mothers never had the chance to decide for themselves if they wanted to be sacrificed on the altar of maternity. Of course, this took place only in extreme cases and today it is rare to encounter such fanaticism, at least in occidental countries. But this choice of child over mother is evident today in even the most moderate Vatican pronouncements, because by denying women the power of choice, and therefore the power to destroy, the Church restricts a woman's function to her reproductive ability. Given the fact that no power is absolutely positive in all its applications, once a woman's power to give life comes

---

27 Betty Friedan, *The Second Stage* (New York: Summit Books, 1981).

without the possibility to control that same power, then all her moral capacities are maintained at their lowest level.

Because the mother is no longer *physically* sacrificed and the destructive effect is internal rather than external, it is thought that Christian morality has evolved in the right direction. But anyone who has ever worked in the area of mental health knows that an imposed pregnancy can cause suffering at every level: psychological, social, economic, intellectual, and spiritual. It is extremely difficult to undergo one or several pregnancies against one's will and still feel like a whole person. Forcing an unwanted pregnancy on a woman is one of the deepest wounds to the spirit that can be inflicted on a human being.

As with slavery, one person controls the body of another and prevents normal relationships from developing with others and with the child. The unwanted child, like the children of slaves, carries the brand of domination even before coming into the world. In the beginning, the Christian Church opposed slavery, and because of this it drew to itself a clientele of slaves. But in practice it has always tolerated and even supported a system of servitude throughout its history. A lord of the Middle Ages did not actually own the serf as a *person* (which is the strict definition of slavery); servitude was defined as the lord owning the *land* on which the serf and his family lived — a circumlocution that allowed Christians to practice slavery in good conscience. The serf and his descendants were attached for life to the master's land; there was no other means of livelihood, no land available not owned by lords, and the serf could neither leave, nor enjoy the fruits of his labor, nor marry without the lord's permission. In some places, the lord even reserved the right to deflower the woman serf on her wedding night .

Practically speaking, the serf found himself in a situation worse than the domestic slaves of Greek and Roman times who at least could eventually be emancipated and produce children who were free. In Rome, for example, under the Empire, the majority of the population were freed slaves. When the Church claims that it did not support slavery, it is a falsehood: it did.[28] But it is also a way of forgetting that it supported servitude, a system considered by many historians to have been worse than slavery.

---

28 The very Catholic Isabelle, Queen of Spain, made a fortune in the trading of slaves with the approval of the Church.

The relationship between serf and lord was the model chosen by the Church to define the relationship between the sexes: a wife must consider her husband to be *lord and master,* which was not then a stylistic device nor a joke but quite literally a form of inequality mandated by the Church. At several points in history, official Christianity has attempted a theological justification of slavery and servitude, arguing that this sort of inequality was as natural as the domination of man over woman (which to them seemed so basic and necessary that no justification was needed). It's a closed circle; sexism and servitude justify each other.

The French historian Guy Fau offers this commentary on the role of official Christianity with respect to women:

> It is not at all paradoxical to recall that at the same time the Church put women back into an inferior status it legitimized slavery, in the name of divine guidance but of course for the benefit of the master. Bossuet only repeated the lessons of St. Augustine, Thomas Aquinas and the Popes when he wrote that to condemn slavery would be to condemn the Holy Spirit which tells slaves, through the words of St. Paul, to be satisfied with their condition and not press their masters to free them. [29]

An unrealistic expectation underlies the prohibition against abortion: a mother must *want* and must *love* all the children she conceives, even when conception is not sought after, even when it is imposed by rape or incest, even when she knows she cannot take on the responsibility. This is an unrealizable expectation because it's an objective that women have *never* been able to attain in all the history of humankind. It is one of those contradictory injunctions that in psychology are known as a double bind, that is, a cruel manipulation that places a person in an impossible situation: no matter what she does or what she feels, she is wrong. If she aborts, she has sinned and is made to feel lacking in generosity, in love, in strength. If she doesn't abort she may not be able to mother the child well because of difficulties resulting from an unwanted pregnancy, and she is then also guilty. She is guilty no matter what she does. This kind of *double bind*, at least as it is described by Gregory Bateson, is more than a contradiction in terms; it carries with it another message, this time addressed to the unconscious, and it enjoins the person not to notice that it is, in fact, a contradictory demand. In other words, it's as if

---

29 Guy Fau, op. cit.

women are told: something impossible is being asked of you, and at the same time you are asked not to realize that the situation is untenable.

The only way out of a double bind is through conscious awareness. One has to become aware of how manipulative, illogical, and crazy the situation is. Religious standards that place women in a double bind destroy them just as surely and in larger numbers as when, for example, a priest refuses to let a doctor perform an abortion that could save the mother's life. The Church has never really accepted the fact that women have souls — souls that suffer.

Even today, the basic fundamentalist position affirms that the fetus is more important than the mother. The choice may no longer be between life and death; it is more likely to be in terms of psychological survival. Just because a wounded spirit is invisible doesn't mean it doesn't exist. The Church will sacrifice the psychological survival of the mother to the fetus every time. If this attitude were limited to the spheres of influence surrounding religious institutions, it would be relatively easy to get rid of; however, for the most part, these Christian values exist on such a subconscious level that we don't even recognize their influence.

Modern obstetrics, for example, without our noticing it, has become a specialty that in its own way sets the child against the mother. The fetus is the true client of obstetricians. One might call them "fetalologist." If a woman complains, for example, about the pressure exerted by a fetal monitor, it is immediately interpreted as self-centeredness. The well-being of the mother is constantly and in the smallest details set against that of the baby, whereas the two are intimately linked.

In the name of avoiding any risk to the fetuses, at least 20% of births are by Caesarean section, a major operation with suffering and risks for the mother, including death. Even if only one in 10,000 dies, if the Caesarean was unnecessary (as is generally the case), are we not on the way to reviving the sacrifice of the mother for the sake of the child? The decision is not made individually at the bedside of each woman, but obstetricians have reclaimed for themselves the Christian standard. And the absurdity of it all is that once the child is born and the woman is barely out of surgery, they send them both home alone without any postnatal care. Women are told that a Caesarean section is better for the baby: "See those lovely little Caesarean babies with nice round heads and no aftereffects of trauma." It's a terrible lie. When a woman is told, "Your baby is going to suffer, we need to do a Caesarean," she accepts right away out of love for her baby and out of fear of the doctors. She accepts being sliced open, needing months to recover from surgery, risking complications and very often postpartum depression because she is so weak. She accepts a huge and permanent scar, missing the important experience of giving birth consciously, for which she has prepared for months, and all of this as a consequent of the Christian medical conspiracy.

Religious attitudes have been translated into medical terms just as they can be found in legal terms. Our doctors along with our judges are still unaware of their religious bias. Their standards go against ecological facts: they deny the basic interdependent link between a woman and her fetus, between the physical and mental well-being of a mother and the quality of the relationship she will establish with her baby, between a couple's joyous experience and the solidarity of the family they will form at the moment of birth. The Christian kingdom is "not of this world," the soul is somewhere up high and the body down below, separated, cut off from each other as spirit from flesh. The body is nothing — only ashes. But these values are disastrous in terms of health. They've also given us a sadistic form of obstetric practice.

Do not disturb

Every time I go to a hotel I can't resist stealing the card from the door handle that says DO NOT DISTURB. To me that is the height of luxury — to be in charge of my time, alone, behind a closed door. My passion for the magic formula printed on the card is a carryover, I believe, from the years when I was constantly trying to balance the need to write, the desire for a profession, and my two children's legitimate need for a mother's attention. But experience has shown me that much more draconian solutions are required than putting signs on doors; a woman has to fight hard for those moments when concentration is possible, because an active woman will always have more responsibilities and things to do than can be contained in one lifetime. Of course, men also have to find ways to avoid frittering away their time, but I think it's more difficult for a woman because a voice inside her tells her repeatedly that her place is with her children, that she is being selfish and irresponsible to want time for herself, to want to succeed professionally, that she will certainly regret it some day when her children mess up their lives.

Contemporary feminism has given autonomy a certain degree of acceptance, but before that it wasn't normal for a woman to want to live alone, to keep a distance socially, just as it is not normal today in the eyes of the pro-life people for a woman not to want to raise all the children that nature sends her. Such a woman aroused suspicion rather than admiration. On the other hand, hermits, wise men, visionaries, or simply loners have often been held up as admirable, and these men are not seen as incomplete just because they decline to be fathers and prefer to be alone. There are few traditions that validate feminine solitude, so that even when a women absents herself for obvious reasons, perhaps to create an original piece of work, her partner, friends, and children are always surprised because it is not a part of the traditional image of femininity.

It is time to call back the image of Artemis, the wild one, who despite her beauty refuses marriage and chooses to belong only to herself. Horsewoman and expert archer, Artemis lives deep in the forest like a hermit who prefers the pleasures of nature to those of the city. The brilliant society of Olympus, the gifts, the intrigues, the ostentatious displays hold no attraction for her. In psychological terms, the image of Artemis represents the *wild side of our psyche*, the part that resists too much socializing and refuses to be completely domesticated. It is that part that makes us want, at certain moments of our lives, to get away from it all, to listen to the wind in the trees, or to an inner voice. Modern psychology, focused as it is on relationships, places little importance on solitude as a factor in mental health. Psychology has affirmed that being present to one's self is a prerequisite to being present to someone else, but has not drawn the obvious conclusion that a good dose of solitude is needed to be present to one's self in the first place. When we are constantly paying attention to another person, to a group, to relatives, colleagues, and friends, how much time, energy, and space are left for this famous being-present-to-one's-self? How much has modern psychology taken Artemis into account?

When the Artemis myth manifests itself in our lives, it can be recognized by a sense of no longer belonging to a group, a couple, or a family; it represents a movement away from what gestalt psychologists call *confluence,* or fusion with others — the most extreme example of fusion being the connection between a mother and her young children. Artemis, unlike the maternal goddesses, invites us to retreat from others, to become autonomous. She is the archetype of those delightful moments when the ego receives no more stimulation and finally quiets down completely.

This benevolent solitude is not to be confused with a depressed withdrawal caused by an isolation experienced as a lack. The isolation of old people or abandoned children or bored teenagers brings them none of the benefits of solitude; they are victims of a situation that deprives them of needed stimulation. Benevolent solitude is an experience of fullness, of peace, whereas isolation is felt as a void. It's accepted that artists, intellectuals, or other recluses need a heavy dose of solitude, but there are many people (who might be called Artemis-type personalities) who need it simply to keep sane. They use it to take walks, to read, to contemplate, or just to think in silence, whether in the country or behind the closed door of an apartment.

When the need for time alone is constantly frustrated, some people can go so far as to lose their balance psychologically. When a woman says that she doesn't want another child because she needs some time for herself, it may not be just a passing notion; the arrival of an unwanted child can bring on a state of despair. One woman might reach this point after raising one child, whereas another may feel perfectly comfortable raising a dozen children who buzz around her like bees in a hive. Each person must learn to interpret the signs that signal the need for space, time, and a body that belongs to no one else. This doesn't mean we should give up important relationships, but everyone can develop the wisdom to recognize that there is a time for fusion and a time for separation. These needs may appear contradictory on the surface but, in reality, they can be attended to alternately.

WOMEN'S STORIES

What do women want?

Josie, a woman of thirty-one, comes to her therapy hour and reports her husband's complaints. He doesn't understand what she wants; one day she wants more intimacy, and the next she says she has no freedom, no time for herself. What, for heaven's sakes, does she really want? More intimacy as a couple or more space for herself? Josie admits she is sending a mixed message to her husband and to her children.

> *Sometimes I seem to be saying "'back off a little so I can breathe'" and then the next day I complain about his being cold and distant and I wish we could spend more time together as lovers. I realize the message is not clear. But I can't seem to make the right connection. You might say I don't know what I want. I want both: I want closer intimacy, and I want more time by myself.*

Her confusion can be explained by the relationship that exists between intimacy and autonomy. True contact, especially between lovers, assumes that the need for autonomy has first been satisfied, that one has "filled up" during moments alone. And, conversely, one cannot be too deficient at the feeling level if solitude is to be truly enjoyable and psychologically safe. In the language of archetypal psychology, we might say Josie is simultaneously deprived of Aphrodite and Artemis. She is missing both the deeply moving connection with her husband (Aphrodite) and the opportunity to get away, to be far from the demands of children and domestic life (Artemis). Her three youngsters, like all normal preschool children, treat her like a domestic commodity. Even if she steals an hour or so at quiet moments of the day, perhaps when the children nap, she always feels like a soldier standing at attention, a sentinel at her post; for twenty-four hours a day she is on maternal duty.

> My attention is always outward. I can't go for a walk, or even read too engrossing a book because it upsets me when I am interrupted every ten minutes. No way can I pursue a train of thought. For me real solitude would be to be guaranteed a full day of not responding to the needs of any other living thing, not even the cat, not even the potted plants.

She is never really alone, and is rarely deeply engaged with her husband. Sometimes she dreams of a more intimate relationship and sometimes of taking off and becoming an Artemisian figure, an unattached virgin, light as a leaping doe and as free as the single student she was before her marriage. Her time would be free, her body free, and her mind free to apply to something that interests her. It's not that her desires are contradictory, but she must make adjustments in time, place, and psychological boundaries in order to live fully these two opposing realities and enjoy the contrast between them.

After several sessions of going over this problem, Josie decided to try the following plan: the children would go to their baby sitter's house for two days a week. The first day, Monday noon through Tuesday noon, would be just for herself, alone in her house, to enjoy peace and quiet. The second day, from Friday noon to Saturday noon, would be time for the couple. They rediscovered the pleasure of making love Saturday morning when they're both well rested and will not be interrupted, and their relationship began to improve. After two months, Josie decided to take a biology course on Monday evenings to see if she was still capable of picking up her studies where she had left off. She followed this regime for three years.

When her youngest child reached school age, Josie was ready, with her husband's support, to study full-time. After a year's work Josie had succeeded so well that her professors recommended her for a scholarship to work towards a master's degree in biology. That's when she realized that she was pregnant with a fourth child despite having faithfully used a diaphragm and contraceptive jelly.

> When the pharmacist told me the test was positive, it was as if I'd been told I would be deprived of oxygen. I felt condemned, and punished for having dared to want to escape my biological role. The whole world seemed to be saying to me: "Don't try to escape, your place is at home until the day you die." I went home and I was obsessed by the memory of a TV program I'd seen as an adolescent. It was called, I think, "The Prisoner." A man was always trying to escape from the place where he was held prisoner. The place, though, was very comfortable, like some first-rate hotel

in the tropics with tennis, pools, splendid accommodations, dining room, and all kinds of services. And yet, in each episode we saw him devising a plan to escape. He always ended up recaptured by a hugh round mass that emerged from the sea, radio-controlled by his jailers, which threatened to smother him if he escaped. The last frame of each episode was of a wrought-iron gate closing on him with the clank of cold metal. That was the image that obsessed me in the drugstore. I thought I could hear the sound of a metal gate closing on me. When I went home to my room and saw my biology books on the desk, I began to cry as if I were about to die. And yet, I never experienced any of that anxiety with my three other children. I had wanted them.

Despite her feminist leanings, despite having always considered abortion a fundamental right, Josie felt overcome with guilt at having an abortion to meet her own needs. And yet the idea of raising another infant and giving up her studies threw her into complete panic. Josie's husband helped her solve the conflict. He did not want a fourth child and clearly desired the abortion. He also didn't want a depressed and defeated wife. After having encouraged her to return to her studies and after collaborating in making it all a success, he would feel let down if she gave up so near the goal, just when a scholarship was possible. He liked her new sense of confidence and didn't want to lose the "new woman" who had succeeded the "housewife/mother." Anyway, if she decided to have a fourth child, he couldn't afford to educate the other three, and he counted on her contribution to relieve the actual burden of his economic responsibilities. Josie had the abortion, but in an extremely conflicted state of mind. She quit therapy.

I did not see her for twelve years, but while writing this book I contacted her to find out if she ever regretted her decision. She now has a doctorate in nutritional science and directs a research lab. Her three children are in college. Here is her response:

No, I never regretted my decision. It was the right one. But one thing I regret terribly — that life is not perfect. There is war, and there is abortion, and there are many other difficult choices. I wanted to have that child and at the same time not lose myself. But it was impossible. A choice had to be made and I made it. But I feel grateful to that little being who only lived in me for three weeks. All the decisions I've made since that time have been made with a different awareness, an awareness that life has its price, my own life included, and that even the life of an aborted fetus may have meaning.

I'm a nutritionist now. I teach courses and give workshops for pregnant women in several hospitals, and I've received an important grant for research in the Third World. It involves improving the diet of pregnant women and newborns in certain areas of Africa, using local products. I will be going there soon. Somehow knowing what my profession cost me has always helped me to give my best and never to accept half-way measures from myself.

My husband had to stop working for three years after the abortion, when I was beginning my doctorate, because he had several successive heart attacks. Perhaps he had felt that a fourth child was beyond his strength? I helped him a lot. I went to work at the same time I was writing my thesis so as to give him a complete rest for two years. He would probably be dead had he not taken those two years to look after himself and make changes in his life. He is now in good shape and is working part-time. Our family is well.

If ever my daughter, or one of my friends, had to choose an abortion, I would try to help her not waste her energy in feeling guilty. I'd try to help her understand that a grown woman who has the ability to choose must never behave like a little girl wanting a doll. I'd tell her that it's often necessary to say "no" to children for their own good. "Charity begins at home" is a maxim that women should take very seriously.

The metaphor of birth

> My body, too, has felt this thrill of pain,
> and I called on Artemis, Queen of the Bow;
> she has my reverence always
> as she goes in the company of the Gods. [30]

Because childbirth is an archetypal experience it is also one of the most meaningful metaphors that represent the torment of creation: we bring forth a book, a painting, a film, a discovery.

Some interpreters of myths have considered Artemis's gynecological function — as protector of women in labor — as an echo of an older pre-Hellenic myth, Cretan perhaps or Asiatic, in which Artemis was one of the manifestations of the goddess mother. But the subsequent evolution of the myth presents an Artemis who never becomes a mother, and is yet continually invoked by women during childbirth. Another way of associating the Virgin with women in labor must be possible, otherwise the mother goddesses (Gaia, Rhea, or Demeter) would have claimed that prerogative. It's true that myths evolve constantly but when a certain representation endures throughout that evolution we can take it to be significant. Therefore there was good reason to see Artemis, the Virgin Queen of animals, as the protector of women in labor. She is also a valid symbol for all those individuals, male and female, who are about to give birth to an important piece of work.

The body of a woman during labor is receiving the most extraordinary level of animal impulses that a human being can experience. It makes sense

---

30 Euripides, *Hippolytus*, 165–68.

then that Artemis was the goddess of childbirth because of her intimacy with nature, with the wilderness, and with female animals. Of all our human experiences childbirth, along with the experience of being born, remains the wildest. (Sexuality can also bring us closer to our animal nature, but this is Dionysos's territory.)

Women who have given birth often say they felt they were battling a ferocious beast who was tearing at their bellies, and that they were in a state of *animal consciousness*. This kind of awareness, personified by Artemis, allows a woman to abandon herself to the powerful work of nature. To resist creates more pain because the contractions, justly termed "labor," become unbearable for a woman who hasn't learned, or doesn't learn under the pressure of the moment, to submit to the attack. Civilized restraint and concern about one's appearance disrupt the movements of a female body in labor. Neither is there a place for emotional hysteria, which is too human an expression and disturbs the beast. Verbal lamentations and tearful supplications are often a sign that something is blocking her ability to concentrate. She is going through the experience like a suffering woman, a tortured human being because many interruptions — technical discussions, ineffective medical procedures, drugs, or the noisy traffic of a typical delivery room — prevent her from concentrating on the rising contractions, as when one gallops forward with ever increasing speed. There's no question of stumbling during this headlong gallop because animal and rider are attached to each other as the soul is to the body. The frightening rhythm will continue to the end, until the child is led to the shore, wet from the crossing, mother and child equally exhausted. Medea spoke for many when she said,

> I would very much rather stand
> Three times in front of battle than bear one child. [31]

The Artemis who rides wild horses and enters into playful combat with animals was my model during labor. I saw her trotting, then galloping, then jumping on the back of a high-spirited horse, and that vision helped me to maintain a level of furious energy up to the time of birth. But these images

---

31 Euripides, *The Medea,* trans. Rex Warner. In *Euripides I,* eds. David Grene and Richmond Lattimore. The Complete Greek Tragedies (Chicago: University of Chicago Press, 1960), 250–51.

appear at other moments as well. Artistic creation, like pregnancy and birth, is an effort of the entire being through which we deliver, in a supreme burst of energy, the product of our gestation — a child or a piece of work. Both require time, so much time that the artist often feels unable to go on, so heavy is she with the work, like a woman in her last month of pregnancy, dragging himself around up until the delivery of the finished piece. In both cases a large dose of patience is needed, and confidence in the natural process of gestation and creation, which for the most part remain below the conscious level. Like a mother, the artist broods over her work with all the love of which she is capable, and her unshakable will turns regularly into a kind of obsession. The artist and the pregnant woman have a physical trait in common — eyes that focus elsewhere, turned towards what is ripening.

The metaphor can be pursued further. The woman giving birth forgets her own culture and is swept along by the primitive force that inhabits her. People knowledgeable about childbirth know that there is this moment, when the baby's head passes through the cervix, that a woman's voice becomes harsh and animal-like, and her cries seem to come from another place, from her animal past. This inhuman cry, experienced by the woman as coming from another, more primitive, personality, is an Artemisian epiphany; untamed nature has taken possession of her. Hermes, the god who opens doors, was also invoked during childbirth, and he plays a role here by facilitating this opening up of the whole being. Once open, no woman has the power to resist pushing the baby out, and it's that push, that strength that we can imagine as belonging to Artemis with her powerful thighs. As soon as the effort has been made and the baby is there, the woman returns to normal consciousness and acquired manners, and then only can she welcome her child with human feeling. Artemis slips back into the depth of the forest.

Is this experience of the wild a valid symbol for artistic creativity? Is giving birth to a work of art all that ferocious? What is the role of the animal spirit in artistic work?

To put forth an exhaustive effort to produce a long-term work requires the participation of the body. That's where the motive power is, in the breath. One feels possessed, seized, eaten by some beast that won't let go until the work achieves the level of perfection of which it's capable. Whatever it is — writing, painting, acting, playing, or composing music, or more prosaically writing a thesis, designing a house, writing up a report, even if it all seems to take little physical energy, even if one is seated for long hours at an intellectual task — the animal is present. It is part of the effort. If we treat it with scorn, it strikes back and makes us ill, dispirited. Or worse yet, it takes off like a cat, fed up at being neglected, leaving us alone, without vitality. Our animal spirit is essential to that hidden kind of intelligence that flows through our body like a carnal memory, and without which there is no creativity. One feels its undeniable presence through tiny pulsations that contain a new idea, the right note, a certain color, the turn of phrase that is exactly right. Our physical reactions serve as a guide and it is through dreams, symptoms, fantasies, and intuitions that the animal spirit teaches us constantly how it wants to be treated if it is to remain our ally. If we fail to pay attention, it threatens us with reprisals. It's difficult to create anything if the body is scorned.

This is what Michelle's dream teaches us, a dream inhabited by a strange beast. At twenty-five, Michelle was enrolled in art school and was beginning a career as a furniture designer. Like Josie, she left it all behind to raise a family. Now that her youngest child is a teenager and she is forty-two, she is offered a chance to pick up her career again, provided she can put together a portfolio showing what she's capable of. Before attacking the portfolio itself, she begins with a few exercises, minor pieces to get her hand back in, to which she accords only bits of time and energy. One morning, full of enthusiasm, she jumps in her car, goes to a bookstore, and comes out with two hundred dollars worth of books with the intention of catching up on her field. She then buys enough artist's supplies in an art store to put together the whole portfolio and more. For a whole week she is intensely absorbed in reading and working to the point of neglecting meals for her family and not answering the phone. She feels seized by a passion more pervasive than sex.

At the same time, she fears it may all become too demanding and her family may suffer, despite repeated encouragement from her husband. A demon whispers in her ear that she is too old, that it's too late to recapture her artistic talent, and that she wasted money on all those purchases. This last was particularly absurd since Michelle is rather extravagant and usually doesn't hesitate to buy what she wants. At the end of that first week, feeling guilty of neglecting her family, she shuts the door of her workshop in the middle of the afternoon, goes to the supermarket, examines carefully the new products and spends the rest of the day preparing an unusually elaborate meal for a weekday. She spends the evening watching TV and goes to bed in a bad mood. This is what she dreams:

> *I dream about a small hungry-looking animal with a face and teeth like a wolf but as small in size as a squirrel. This creature clings to a branch of a very old tree in the forest where I am walking. It's dusk and there's not much light. Despite the darkness I go towards the tree and look up to the branch where the animal is watching me. As soon as I look directly into its eyes it jumps gracefully onto my shoulder and fastens on me as if I were a branch. I'm scared. I figure there's no way to dislodge it because it's not only attached with its feet but it has me by the neck, its teeth ready to tear out my jugular vein. I know it won't bite me if I go along with it. Intuitively, as if controlled from within by signals from the animal, I return home to the door of my workshop, and I understand then very clearly that I must go to work immediately and continue until I have recovered all my artistic powers. Then only will the animal let go, without hurting me in any way. But if I refuse, his teeth will sink into my neck and I will bleed to death.*

Michelle concluded from this dream that she had no choice; either she would give birth to a portfolio or she would lose her vitality. She got back to work seriously and within six months she completed her portfolio. Unfortunately, it was too late to get the job she wanted, but she became an artist again and was confident about finding another job. That opportunity came a year later after displaying some of her work in a neighborhood cultural center. The dream-animal had been a guide — a messenger from Artemis.

Once the work is finished every artist feels emptied and exhausted like the new mother who, still bloodied, sweaty, and dry-mouthed, sips orange juice before falling back on the pillow. Apollo, the god most often associated with intellectual achievement, is certainly not the only archetype to influence the creative spirit. Variations in personality can explain why artists develop differing relationships to the intellect, with more or less importance accorded to Artemis or to Apollo. But the artist influenced by Artemis reveals a certain indifference to the work once it is produced; society's acceptance is of no particular interest since she works at her art because she needs to do it. She can no more stop her flow of self-expression than a woman can stop a child from being born. The artist who denies her art does it at the risk of pain and neurosis. No outward display, no mannerisms, no sentimentality for the creator either; she must ride her imagination at a gallop and not miss a beat.

Childbirth and artistic creation reflect the two poles of nature — the generosity that creates life and the harshness that devastates and sometimes kills the body or the soul. Dreams in which a pregnant woman sees herself dying seem to derive from the same archetypal reality. One might say medicine has changed things and today few women die giving birth. The time is also past when artists almost starved themselves to buy their tubes of paint. And yet, the fear of annihilation felt by the artist and the pregnant woman still exists. A doctor can show a woman all kinds of statistics to prove she has nothing to worry about, and an artist may be privately wealthy and never lack for anything, but the basic anxiety will not change because alongside physical destruction there is the failure of a personality to express itself — the death of soul. Some women, after the birth of a child, only survive as someone's mother: the virginal identity, the sense of autonomy can be wiped out, and those who are not aware of this risk are simply naive. Many pregnant women sense this danger, which is the source of their fear. When a woman says she doesn't want a child because she isn't ready and needs first to develop her own personality, she is not being capricious. Her life is at stake, and even if an unwanted pregnancy doesn't threaten her life physically, she could harm herself another way. The destruction of the soul is not visible, but it is just as real as the destruction of the body. Surviving with a broken spirit is not really living.

The cure for guilt

Just as cleaning up contamination won't be enough to create an ecological balance, decriminalizing abortion has not brought us a society that's aware of its reproductive power. We need to invent rituals, think up symbols, propose new ideas, and create a network of support for women and couples so that they can make the decision in a guilt-free state of mind. Contraceptive failure is a mistake, but it is not a moral lapse; there is no wrongful intent.

I received a call one day from a young man, a former university student who asked for a psychological consultation. He wanted to bring along his girlfriend who had just left an abortion clinic. Neither of them regretted their decision, and all had gone well. But she felt extremely "bizarre" about going back to the office the next day as if nothing had happened. For an hour they discussed their decision. They felt too young to raise children since they were still economically dependent on their own parents; they were also uncertain about their fairly new relationship and anxious to develop their professional skills so as to be independent of their families; eventually they wanted a family, children, a home, but right now a baby would be a catastrophe.

Finally, as it became more and more evident that this couple had made the right decision, one they were happy with, I suggested they go to a very good restaurant since the girl had been fasting since the night before. There was *reason to celebrate:* they had successfully made their first decision as a couple conscious of its reproductive power. Several days later the girl called me. She wanted me to know that for the first time in her life she had understood how wonderful it was to live in a country where democracy and feminism had made their mark. Democracy for her was just an abstraction, and feminism seemed a bit outdated. She loved the young man and didn't want to damage their chance to have a family. Our talk had allowed them to grasp the seriousness of creative power and to celebrate the awareness with which they had exercised that power.

Our culture needs new rituals as well as laws to restore to abortion its sacred dimension, which is both terrible and necessary. In too many cases a woman goes through a clinic like a car going in for an oil change, and the fetuses are put in the trash. The whole process, like birth, follows a medical model, but the wound to the soul remains untreated. In some hospitals, abortions are done in assembly-line fashion. Sometimes the only communication between doctor and patient is to make sure she has been fasting. The usual hospital procedure requires the patient to be lying on her back, legs apart, while she waits for the doctor. He opens the cervix, a procedure that often provokes a flood of emotion for which the woman is unprepared; the suction pump is placed and activated, and it's over. The ritual may vary in detail, but its chief characteristic is to be as fast as possible. This may be adequate for the clinical part, but what becomes of fear, guilt, and sorrow? Guilt can be crushing and unjust in the sense that women alone bear a burden that belongs to everyone. She goes home and cries and holds her belly. Some women are tempted to hide out long enough to try to get rid of feelings of shame and guilt which run counter to their conscious reasoning but which they feel nevertheless. With whom do they share this event? There are no priests, still less priestesses, to grant them absolution. The luckier ones will have the support of the man who got them pregnant, a friend, a mother, a therapist, or a friendly medical team. Some clinics offer a network of psychological support (group meetings or one-to-one) and arrange the environment, the pace of operations and the relationships in a way that allows women to be heard, absolved, pardoned and supported. But many go through the experience alone. Even worse, some are condemned by the people around them including their own mothers.

How should a woman comport herself before, during, and after this important event? Such questions are generally left unanswered in a kind of cultural and religious void that puts the guilt and sorrow on the woman, the couple, and perhaps the parents, without support from society at large, still dominated by Christian values. Most women who choose abortion love children and are tempted, often unconsciously in an animal way, to keep it. But it is through consciousness, a feminine consciousness, that they choose not to give birth.

A ritual that is well adapted to the circumstance can help them feel the love, the sadness, and the regret associated with an interruption of pregnancy. I've heard women address their fetus directly, with a therapist or in a support group, and explain why it is necessary to separate now. Others write a letter of farewell and read it to a friend, a spouse, or indeed to their whole family. Still others invent their own farewell ritual, inspired perhaps by rituals from other cultures, like offering a little doll to a divinity as a symbol of the aborted fetus.

In addition to saying goodbye, a woman may need to talk about how she will focus the energy that will not be devoted to another pregnancy. A woman is often conscious of having something to contribute. What is that other task that she wants to accomplish? Why does it seem more important to her than continuing with her pregnancy? To what ideal or what set of values is she sacrificing this fetus? It's useful to think it through and communicate it to someone else. This is where a group, a ritual, can help, along with an atmosphere that allows ritual to have its beneficial effect. I won't deny that some women are selfishly motivated since there is egoism in all kinds of decisions, even in the decision to have the child (who is then a doll, a compensation, a weapon in the marital relationship, a trophy, a proof of one's fertility, a projection of one's ambition). But giving thought to a career is not necessarily a selfish act.

If a young woman aborts before she has had a child, it may be helpful for her shortly after to spend time holding a baby in her arms, cradling it, and feeling the special beauty of a newborn. Some teenagers believe that having an abortion is a sign that one will not be a good mother! It helps them to think of *abortion as a maternal decision*, a mother's responsibility — the first a woman has to make, often without any previous experience of maternity. This is why it's important not to be cut off from babies if one aborts for the first time and has never given birth. In the same way, accident victims are advised to get back into their cars as soon as possible so as not to develop a fear that increases with time.

Abortion is a heartbreak.

It's like other life experiences, when we're confronted with an impossible love or a broken friendship, sacrificed for the sake of reason or necessity. The pain of having to say no is the same. We feel we could have loved, could still love that person for the rest of our lives but it just isn't possible. In almost all cases, the aborted fetus represents an impossible love. It's rare for a woman to choose abortion because in some way she dislikes the fetus. She sacrifices it for the sake of something she judges at this moment to be more important, whether it be her existing children — children she will have one day, her own physical, economic, or psychological survival, or the fate of the planet.

A friend offered me her testimony when she learned I was writing this book. Seven years after an abortion, she decided to write down her experience in detail and allowed me to add it to this chapter. Her profession is midwifery.

Farewell, my love

> *When I awoke that morning with a prickly feeling in the tips of my breasts and a subtle heaviness in my lower belly I already knew I was pregnant. It was the first time it had happened when I didn't want it to happen. I thought about nothing else night and day for two weeks. I wanted to weigh everything, think of everything, all the alternatives, all the angles, taking into account the energy, the support, and the money that was available or even possible. No matter how I looked at it I came to the same conclusion: alone with two children, with no help from their father, I could accept a third child only through some dubious and costly form of heroism on my part. I would be giving life at the cost of swallowing up what little energy is left over from my job. I would be giving life to the detriment of my two small children who still need me a lot. And finally I would lose the creative momentum in the work that I adore, the work that nourishes me, the work that was then and still is my contribution to the world. So the decision was clear, the appointment was made, and yet I was inconsolable. Several times a day, at the most unexpected moments, I was overcome with tears that I had more and more difficulty hiding from or justifying to my two children who were too young to understand. My heart was broken.*

Paradoxically, during this period of reflection and calculation, my heart went about doing what it had done for my other children, loving this little creature curled up somewhere in my belly. I had long silent conversations with it. Why had it come? Why the absurd contraceptive failure? And above all why these waves of love for it, just as I was getting ready to refuse it a place, and thereby a life? The waves of love were so physical they were beyond my control; they submerged me every day in a painful and sensual way, like inflows of milk. I could only let myself glide along, feverish and amorous, full but without roundness yet, a little intoxicated as at the beginning of an affair. So why refuse all that? The absurd tearing apart of the abortion process seemed intolerable. I had to find an answer in the deepest part of my being.

During one of those inexplicable loving conversations I felt as if I was carrying in me someone who had previously died in complete oblivion, anonymously, far from loved ones. And that it had come this time to refashion its departure from life. Just the departure. But this time in full and loving consciousness. And I could give that. I don't know where the idea came from, nor is it important; it gave meaning to what I was going through and allowed me to commit myself whole-heartedly to my decision and to my love.

Which I did, right up to the night before the appointment. The separation approached and wrung my heart. I cried so much that evening I thought a dam had burst. I asked myself: "What am I crying about? The death of a fetus? My own cruelty? A child I'll never know?" The friend who offered me a shoulder to cry on assured me the answer was not important, that I just needed to let myself feel the pain. But I felt I might find a clue in that answer. I suddenly realized through my tears that I was afraid of being a bad mother to this baby. But bad mothers, if they exist at all, don't worry about harming their little ones. No, I wasn't a bad mother. On the contrary I was giving this creature the best of me, as I had done for the other two. All of this came to me with such certainty that a great sense of peace ran through me and I went to sleep with only a few leftover sobs.

I woke up in the same frame of mind, calm, sad and serene.

When my turn came I stretched out on the table, feet in the stirrups, ready to let my little darling go. But as soon as the doctor touched my cervix with the first metal instrument I became terribly nauseated and drenched in sweat; everything toppled over backwards, the whole room went dark. They began to throw cold water in my face, check my blood pressure, call out to me, while I put my total effort into each breath so as not to lose contact. I was in a state of clinical shock, my body reacting violently to what it perceived as mortal danger. I wondered for a long time afterward why that had happened when I had been so at peace with my decision. I realized that even if my head and my heart accepted the loss, my uterus still saw it as a mortal threat and was protesting with all its strength in an effort to protect its little lodger. I was very proud of my uterus for doing its job so well!

After everything calmed down the procedure moved gently ahead. One instrument, then another. Breathe, breathe, breathe. Say yes, say yes. And when the machine made its horrible, absurd noise I talked to it: "Farewell. Goodbye, my beautiful little love." And I cried. Then the machine shut off. It was over. My baby was really gone. The rest of the day went by smoothly, my hands on my belly for warmth, and a kind of muted pain or the memory of pain. A few tears of sorrow now and then. Only sorrow.

The next day life went back to normal. But curiously several friends I met asked me: "What's going on with you? You're so radiant today, you're absolutely glowing." What's going on is that I've just had an abortion and lived an impossible love and accomplished a great reconciliation with myself. But it was my secret and my gift.

Now seven years later I cry as I write this. Not with regret, or remorse or guilt. Just tears of sadness. My darling is still alive but he is far away. And I am its mother.

Not sinful: stupid!

When the Greek or Latin poets make the gods talk they often deplore human folly. The divinities complain that humans are so proud, so jealous, so uncontrolled in their ambitions that they have to get angry and impose some order so as to make humans experience the results of their stupidity! So when pagans were faced with epidemic, famine, madness, or nightmares, they asked themselves questions like these: which god or goddess have we offended by our behavior? Why are we being punished? What foolishness on our part could bring about such a calamity? These questions may sound like superstition, but it's a way of speaking through images. The ancient Greeks took their divinities with a much larger grain of salt than was used to season our catechism! Today we use another vocabulary. We ask ourselves: What's my problem? Where does my neurosis come from? What values am I neglecting? Where does this psychosomatic symptom come from? Instead of saying, "I'm sick because I eat poorly and get no exercise," the ancient Greek would have developed the same idea, saying, "I'm sick because I offended Demeter [the goddess of nourishment]. Or because I don't honor the god of sport [that could mean Artemis in the case of an adolescent girl, or Hermes, or Apollo, depending on the context]." In other words, visualizing the anger of a god was a way of acknowledging the foolishness of an act by holding it against an important standard that one persists in neglecting.

In our present culture, it is neither a sin nor, for now, against the law to pollute the little stream on my property, to clear-cut the forest, to transform a park into a parking lot. By the same token, the unemployment rate among the young, the suffering of abandoned children, and the isolation of old people do not appear as sins in any present religious code. Yet those who are aware of a larger global picture know that something very serious is happening. The error is a serious one, we feel it as such, not as a sin but as an unacceptable unbelievable stupidity. Here the ecologist and the pagan would agree: it's not a question of sin, just stupidity. The pagan value judgement is

not based on a dogma that forbids this or that but on the practical consequences of an act.

Abortion has been judged up to now according to Christian dogma; it's a
sin because it is forbidden by the Church, and the Church cannot change its
position because it is written in the Bible and if we begin to change written
dogma the whole religion would collapse. Monotheistic religions, which are
based on a book (the Bible, the Torah, or the Qu'ran), function according to
written laws (dogma) that divide behavior into sin and virtue, once and for
all. But as soon as we adopt a more global and less dogmatic perspective, we
can see the foolishness of sacrificing the mother for the baby, the stupidity of
obstetric procedures that only consider the comfort and safety of the fetus
(as if mother and child were not interdependent), and the folly of a moral
stance that forces women to have children when the first need of a child is
to be wanted.

Shame and guilt

Sin carries with it a guilty feeling, whereas stupidity provokes a sense of
shame. When a sin is confessed, penance is done, and that's that. It's the same
with infractions of the civil code; one is pronounced guilty, one pays his debt
to society, and we're all even again. But when you've done something stupid
you feel ashamed, sheepish. Shame is an inner experience, connected to our
deepest being; this is why it provokes uncontrollable physiological reactions
like blushing. The anthropologist E. R Dodds[32] makes a fundamental distinction between a culture based on shame, generally an oral culture, and one
based on guilt, with a written code of law and a judicial system to enforce it.
In a guilt culture, one may think there's no wrong done if one is not caught,
and no shame either. But this distinction is never absolute; abortion, for example, involves an intermingling of the two. Even though it is no longer a
criminal act, women who abort experience both shame and guilt.

Shame always expresses the values transmitted to us by our culture. It
springs up every time we think we've mocked some standard of behavior
that's important to us or to the community around us. We can't eliminate
feelings of shame, but a shift in emphasis is possible. All cultures use shame

---

32 E. R. Dodds. *The Greeks and the Irrational* (Berkeley: University of California Press,
1962), chapter 2 ("From Shame-Culture to Guilt-Culture").

for many kinds of indispensable training: a child, for example, has to understand, no matter how skillfully the incident is handled, that a certain amount of disgrace is attached to peeing on the living room rug, to disobeying the proprieties of living in society. Shame and guilt are unavoidable in the educational process. But the social consensus needs to be re-examined at regular intervals and questions asked again and again: where does *that* shame come from? Is it really shameful not to mow my lawn? Should I be ashamed if I'm not a financial success? Is it shameful to be fat, ugly, old, or alone? To be a young boy and have a visible erection at the beach? To be illiterate, to belong to an ethnic group judged to be inferior? To have an irritating accent? To see my mother make a social blunder?

Should a university student be ashamed of not understanding a phrase like "historical reductionism is only the contradictory exclusion of formalist reduction," so ashamed that she does not dare open her mouth for a whole semester?

What was I ashamed of, twenty years ago, during a department meeting I was chairing, when I noticed that milk was seeping from my breasts, making an increasingly large circle on the front of my blouse? What exactly was I ashamed of? Of pretending to be an intellectual while having the breasts of a nursing mother? Of being a woman?

Psychology is helpful in treating shame on an individual basis, in asking, "What standard of values do I respect, and what do I see as a destructive kind of prejudice?" Therapy tries to help us see if there's agreement between our accepted values and our feelings. Christianity taught us to be ashamed of our bodies, of some of our emotions, of femininity, and many therapists are busy treating the embarrassment that lingers in the subconscious even when we think we've rid ourselves of old religious strictures. But in the collective unconscious, the job is only half done. For example, I wonder why rapists are not ashamed. This fact is one of the mysteries in the treatment of violent men; they are not ashamed of their violence. Why aren't the big industrial polluters ashamed? And big-time financial crooks? And lying politicians? Shame seems to be pathologically absent in many contemporary settings, and abundant in others.

A *pagan ecology* could provide a new perspective on shame on the collective level just as psychotherapy can help us defuse it on the personal level. When we abandoned traditional religious standards, we believed that a civil code, a system based on legal proceedings, proof of guilt and punishment, would be enough to maintain collective values. But a law forbidding the pollution of streams will never suffice if the perpetrator feels no shame, if he doesn't feel *personally tarnished* at the thought of throwing garbage into pure water. If we rely solely on laws and regulations, we'll need video cameras behind every tree to *catch* the person in the act. And all these large-scale polluters, owners of industries, and legislators will continue to display the same pathological absence of shame. We'll come to a legislative dead end.

Polluters aware of what they're doing are similar in psychological make-up to men convicted of domestic violence. These men readily admit what they've done; they know they're guilty of breaking the law. But for them the law is a little like the speed limit on the highway. It's an annoyance. It would be so much better to drive your car as fast as it will go, and beat your wife and children when you feel like it. Being restricted, being caught and punished, is what bothers them deeply, but they feel no shame. For them domestic violence, pollution, and exceeding the speed limit are all the same thing. In the same kind of mind frame, it doesn't occur to these people that their avoidance of environmental controls have made them more isolated human beings.

It's foolish to want to eliminate feelings of shame because they signal the internalization of a moral value. But we must constantly monitor the values attached to shame, as we educate the next generation, so that it can be put aside when it no longer expresses our ideals and can be revived when it appears to be pathologically absent. The shame felt after an abortion should be part of this re-evaluation. When an abortion is necessary, not only should there be no shame, but there should be a new consensus that to have a child who cannot adequately cared for is shameful.

Women and girls, universally associated with nature, inevitably become "rape-able," usable in a culture that fails to value what Artemis represents. The philosopher Mary Daly, a feminist of Artemisian intransigence, by analogy with the Indian caste system, speaks of women as an international caste of "touchables."[33] When a culture refuses to recognize the inherent value of a woman, when her worth is measured as it relates to another value, the child or the man, self-awareness is perceived as an absence, according to Daly,

33 Mary Daly. *Pure Lust: Elemental Feminist Philosophy* (Boston: Beacon Press, 1984).

since the woman can only be seen in the context of her relative usefulness. In that context, she says, women are touchable, natural resources are exploit-able, girls are rape-able, and children can be mistreated.

Some part of nature and some part of womanhood must remain virgin. One must preserve in one's self, whether man or woman, an intact strength, inviolable and radically feminine; this is the Artemisian part of the anima that guards the untamed zone of our psyche, without which we risk becoming overdomesticated human beings, too easily touchable.

This same quality allows us to visualize a world of increasing respect for children — a world in which one can occasionally resort to abortion when it is necessary to sacrifice the fetus to a higher cause, namely, the love of chil-dren and the refusal to see them suffer.

Abortion as a sacrifice to Artemis. Abortion as a sacrament — for the gift of life to remain pure.

ABOUT THE AUTHOR

GINETTE PARIS is core faculty and research coordinator in the Mythologi-
cal Studies Program and Research Coordinator at Pacifica Graduate In-
stitute in Carpinteria, Calif. She is the author of *Pagan Meditations* and *Pagan
Grace*. Her forthcoming book, *Depth Psychology after Neuroscience: Wisdom, Psyche,
and the Humanities,* will be published by Routledge in July 2007.